Secret Beaches
Southwest England

First published by *Secret Seeker*, an imprint of One More Grain Of Sand, 2011
This 2nd edition published by *Secret Seeker*, an imprint of One More Grain Of Sand, 2015
info@onemoregrainofsand.com

www.secretseeker.com

Research, cartography and photography by Rob Smith
Additional photography by Brendan Barry
Book design by Ben Hoo, Simon Borrough and Rob Smith
Book series design by Ben Hoo
Edited by Rufus Purdy and Jo Kirby
Printed by Cambrian Printers, Aberystwyth, Wales

ISBN: 978-1-910992-05-0

Photo credits: Brendan Barry on p.10, 62, 106, 142, 174, 251 (sunsets & seclusion), 252 (long hikes), 253 (families & short walks), 254; Jane Sarchet on p.252 (pubs).

Help us update: A great deal of effort and many pints of Doom Bar went into the making of this book, but if you think something could be improved, an instruction could be clearer or you find the perfect pitstop to include in the next edition, we'd love to hear from you: info@onemoregrainofsand.com

Publisher's note: Many of the walks within this publication follow steep, rocky pathways. Every effort has been made to provide sufficient warning where necessary and also grading of the beach-access routes, which can be seldom used and are susceptible to erosion. The publisher and author accept no responsibility for injuries or deaths that arise from following the suggested routes to access the beaches featured in this book. You are responsible for your own safety. You should rely on your own assessment of whether a particular route is suitable for your abilities or whether it has deteriorated to a point where it is no longer safe to use. Coastal swimming is also hazardous. Make sure you inform yourself correctly about rip tides or other dangers before entering the water.

ONE
MORE
GRAIN
OF
SAND

Secret Beaches: Southwest England began life back in 2002 as a small map with a long name: *The West Cornwall Aerial Photography Map of Secluded Beaches and Hidden Coves*. I'd heard rumours of the county's secret beaches and was determined to put my new-found cartography skills to use in mapping them. Just as I was about to embark on the project, though, I broke my right ankle in a climbing accident and – a few weeks later, after the cast had been removed – seriously twisted the other. A physiotherapist friend recommended gentle country walking. 'Uneven ground,' she said, 'is key to recovery.'

Convinced that researching the map would be perfect for my recuperation, I set off for Cornwall to test my tendons on the Southwest Coastal Path. I quickly forgot I was under orders to take it easy and took the 'uneven ground' advice to its limits by walking for miles up and down headlands each day. The project was a success, but it whetted my appetite to produce something bigger: a book that incorporated all 1,105 kilometres of the Southwest Coastal Path. And this time I was going to come up with a snappier title.

Secret Beaches: Southwest England would not have been possible without the effortless good nature of the people who helped me along the way: farmers opening their fields for me to camp in; chance meetings that became spontaneous guided tours; casual conversations that led me down seldom-trodden paths. People of the southwest, I salute you.

I hope you love visiting the beaches in this book as much as I've done. And so in the spirit of the research and all those who helped me with it, let's take responsibility for these beaches. Let's help those who doggedly clean up the unending tide of flotsam that washes up on the shores. Even picking up a few extra plastic bottletops along with your own rubbish will make a difference. You'll be making the beaches even more beautiful. They're yours to enjoy now, after all...

HOW TO USE THIS BOOK

We hope you'll find *Secret Beaches: Southwest England* easy to use. To get to any of the beaches we've included, simply follow our Getting There directions or type the car park postcode into your SatNav device. And, once you're in situ, the map and numbered walking instructions will guide you along the suggested route. Here's how we've rated our beaches and walks:

WALK INFORMATION

These details are for your reference, and will enable you to judge whether the walk we've suggested is within your capabilities.

BH20 5BJ

The nearest postcode for the car park or parking area at the start of the walk to the beach.

THE WALK
1km / 20mins

Walk classification: Easy (E), Moderate (M) or Hard (H). A short walk that includes a very steep hill will be classed as Hard, while a long walk over flat, undemanding terrain will be classed as Moderate. Distance: given in kilometres. Time: how long it would take someone to travel across rough terrain at average walking speed with no stops.

BEACH
ACCESS

Beach access classed as Easy, Moderate, Hard or Extreme (X). A beach might be easy to get to, but if the access pathway down to it from the headland is long and steep, with a sheer drop on one side, we've classed it as Hard. Take great care when descending to beaches listed as Extreme.

BEACH QUALITY RATINGS

We've rated the different aspects of the beaches from 1 to 5 – with 5 being the best or highest rating.

SUNBATHING

A high rating here means you should expect soft golden sand, smooth comfortable shingle or level, grassy headland to lounge upon.

SECLUSION

A rating of 5 here means you're unlikely to see anyone else on the shore, except on the very hottest, sunniest summer days.

5 SWIMMING

A rating of 5 here means the beach slopes gently into the sea. WARNING: Always inform yourself about offshore currents when swimming in the sea.

5 SAND

A rating of 5 here means there is soft, golden sand to enjoy. A beach will also rate highly here if it offers small, smooth, comfortable pebbles.

5 ROCKPOOLS & CAVES

A rating of 5 here means the beach is home to plenty of rockpools that are ideal for crabbing, etc. A beach will also rate highly if there are some great caves to explore nearby.

BEACH INFORMATION

A tick or a cross indicates whether the following is permitted or possible.

NATURISM

DOGS ALLOWED

SURF

MAP KEY

○	Walk start/finish point	Ⓣ	Public toilets		Walk shortcut / Optional extra walk
➋	Walk direction number		Walk route		Secret beach
ⓟᵤᵦ	Pub/Inn		Road/lane		Other beach
Ⓟ	Car park		Pathway		Land
Ⓒ	Café/Tea room		River/stream		Sea

SECRET SEEKER APP

Launching summer 2020, our new mobile app *SECRET SEEKER* will enable you to follow the walking routes in this book on your smartphone and leave the book at home. All the maps, walk directions and other route information will be there for you to follow. Check our website in spring 2018 for latest news on the app and its expected launch date: **www.secretseeker.com**

secret seeker

CONTENTS

Land's End & The Lizard

		page
01	The Helford Estuary	14
02	Lankidden & Downas Coves	22
03	Lizard Point	26
04	Rinsey Beach	34
05	Porth Chapel	38
06	Nanjizal	42
07	Gwynver	46
08	Portheras Cove	50
09	Porthmeor Cove	54
10	Veor Cove	58

North Cornwall

11	Fishing Cove	66
12	Porth Joke	70
13	Diggory's Island Sand	74
14	Fox Cove	78
15	Doom Bar	82
16	Tregardock Beach	90
17	Benoath Cove	94
18	The Strangles	98
19	Stanbury Mouth	102

North Devon

20	Welcombe & Marsland Mouths	110
21	Berry Beach	114
22	Mouthmill Beach	118
23	Rockham Beach	122
24	Lee Bay	126
25	Wild Pear Beach	130
26	Woody Bay	134
27	Wringcliff Bay	138

South Cornwall

		page
28	Molunan	146
29	Porthbeor Beach	150
30	Booley Beach	154
31	Great Lantic Beach	158
32	Frog Prince Cove	162
33	Donkey Beach	166
34	Polhawn Cove	170

South Devon

35	Swaney Cove	178
36	Meadowsfoot Beach	182
37	Westcombe Beach & Ayrmer Cove	186
38	Avon Estuary	190
39	Soar Mill Cove	194
40	Prawle Point	198
41	Great Mattiscombe Sand	204
42	Landcombe Cove	208
43	Castle & Compass Coves	212

Jurassic Coast

44	Littlecombe Shoot	220
45	Hooken Beach	224
46	Cogden Beach	228
47	White Nothe Beach	232
48	Mupe Bay	236
49	Chapman's Pool	240
50	Shipstal Beach & the Arne Nature Reserve	244

Index		248
Best Beaches For...		250

Atlantic
Ocean

Cornwall

English
Channel

Ilfracombe
Woolacombe
Croyde
Barnstaple
Bideford
Hartland
Bude
Holsworthy
Hatherleigh
Okehampton
Crackington Haven
Tintagel
Launceston
Rock
Padstow
Bodmin
Saltash
Plymouth
Ivybri
Newquay
Perranporth
St. Austell
Looe
Truro
Mevagissey
Redruth
St. Ives
Gwithian
Hayle
Falmouth
St. Just
Penzance
Helston
Gweek
Lizard

26
25
24
23
22
21
20
19
18
17
16
15
14
13
12
11
10
09
08
07
06
05
04
01
02
03
29
28
30
31
32
33
34
35
36
37
38
39

N

27

Minehead

Bridgwater   Glastonbury

Somerset

nton

Taunton

Tiverton   Yeovil

th Molton

Devon

Dorset

Exeter
                                  Seaton Lyme Regis   Bridport
Sidmouth 44 45   46   Dorchester   Poole
Exmouth   50
                                                                          Wareham
                                              Weymouth   47   48   Swanage
Newton Abbot   49

Torquay

Totnes

Dartmouth 43
42
ngsbridge

40 41

Land's End & The Lizard
Beaches 1 to 10   Pages 10 to 61

North Cornwall
Beaches 11 to 19   Pages 62 to 105

North Devon
Beaches 20 to 27   Pages 106 to 141

South Cornwall
Beaches 28 to 34   Pages 142 to 173

South Devon
Beaches 35 to 43   Pages 174 to 215

Jurassic Coast
Beaches 44 to 50   Pages 216 to 247

Land's End &
The Lizard

Atlantic Ocean

Navax Point

The Island

St. Ives Bay

Gwi

St. Ives

Zennor

Hayle

Morvah

Cornwall

Cape Cornwall

St. Just

Penzance

St. Michael's Mount

Whitesand Bay

Mount's Bay

Land's End

Sennen

Porthcurno

Land's End & The Lizard

		Page
01	The Secret Coves of the Helford Estuary	14
02	Lankidden & Downas Coves	22
03	The Sequestered Sands of Lizard Point	26
04	Rinsey Beach	34
05	Porth Chapel	38
06	Nanjizal	42
07	Gwynver	46
08	Portheras Cove	50
09	Porthmeor Cove	54
10	Veor Cove	58

Porthreath

Truro

Redruth

Camborne

Nare
Head

Penryn

St. Mawes

Falmouth

Zone
Point

Camborne

Falmouth
Bay

Porth Nanvas

Helston

01

Gweek

Helford

English
Channel

Mullion

02

Black
Head

Lizard

03

Lizard
Point

N

The Secret Coves of the Helford Estuary

Somerset

Devon

Dorset

Cornwall

Tucked beneath the arm of the expansive, ship-teeming mouth of the River Fal, the Helford Estuary is a small, perfectly formed area of rock-and-sand shores and forested banks that slinks its way across the top of the Lizard peninsula. Famed for its beauty and tranquillity, as well as its thriving wildlife – which includes some of Britain's finest oysters – it is an ideal spot from which to enjoy the sunset. Find yourself a good vantage point and watch the way crimson light splits into shards as it bounces off the surface of streams that curl inland through wooded valleys. The coves found here bear few traces of the modern world, and are sure to instil a love of nature in even the most hardened city-dweller. Our two suggested walks take in both shores of the estuary, and pass through some of the most secluded and beautiful beaches in the UK.

North Shore
TR11 5LD

South Shore
TR12 6JX

E

THE WALKS
6km (north)
5km (south)

E

BEACH
ACCESS

NORTH SHORE GETTING THERE

– Head west out of Falmouth and follow signs to Porth Navas. When you reach Helford Passage, look out for the car park (postcode: TR11 5LD).

1 Our suggested route is approximately six kilometres long. But it passes five beaches, so you can stop at any of these to cut the walk short.

2 To begin, walk down the hill from the car park, turning left onto the Coastal Path when you reach the shore. All of the beaches can be accessed from this winding track.

3 You will come across the first beach, Passage Cove, almost immediately. Our suggested North Shore pitstop, The Ferryboat Inn, is located here; as is the ferry pontoon that takes you across to the South Shore.

SOUTH SHORE GETTING THERE

– Head west on the A394 to Helston, then follow signs to Helford. When you arrive in the village, park in the easy-to-find car park (postcode: TR12 6JX).

1 Once again, our suggested route – around five kilometres this time – can be shortened if you stop at a beach closer to the starting point.

2 Take the path from the car park, and walk along the shore through woodland that offers snapshot glimpses of the estuary through trees.

3 All four beaches are adjacent to this track. Simply walk out of the woods onto the sand.

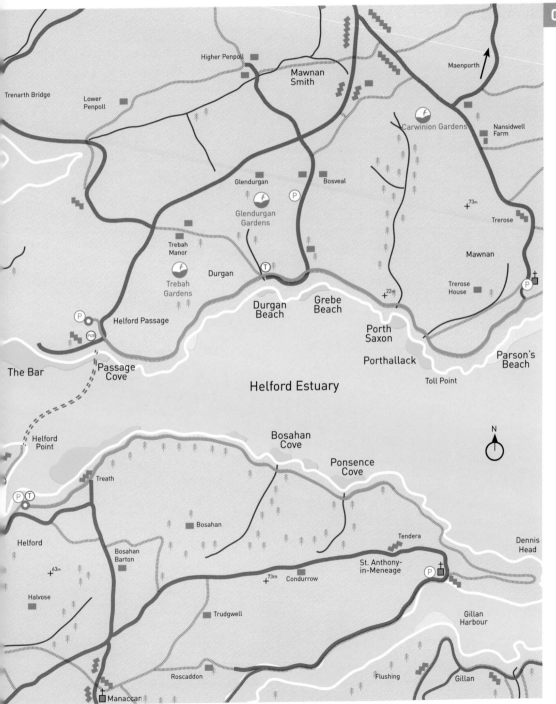

Trenarth Bridge

Lower Penpoll

Higher Penpoll

Mawnan Smith

Maenporth

Carwinion Gardens

Nansidwell Farm

Glendurgan

Bosveal

+73m

Trerose

Glendurgan Gardens

P

Trebah Manor

T

Mawnan

Durgan

Trerose House

Trebah Gardens

Durgan Beach

Grebe Beach

+22m

P

Helford Passage

P

PUB

Porth Saxon

Parson's Beach

The Bar

Passage Cove

Porthallack

Toll Point

Helford Estuary

Helford Point

Bosahan Cove

N

Ponsence Cove

Treath

Dennis Head

P T

Bosahan

Tendera

Helford

Bosahan Barton

+63m

St. Anthony-in-Meneage

P

Halvose

+73m

Condurrow

Gillan Harbour

Trudgwell

Roscaddon

Flushing

Gillan

Manaccan

NORTH SHORE THE BEACHES

A backdrop of open countryside and a south-facing shoreline means that the estuary's northern beaches are slightly more popular than those on the opposite side of the water. Strewn with tiny, barefoot-friendly pebbles and surrounded with dense, almost tropical-looking foliage, they are all wonderful places from which to go swimming. Stroll along a path that rolls out over gentle, grassy hills, occasionally dipping into woodland and streams, and tarry at your leisure. First comes Passage Cove and Durgan Beach, then Grebe Beach, the largest of our suggested stops, which sits in front of an ancient village of eerily small houses. After Grebe come the twin beaches of Porth Saxon and Porthallack, both of which are as beautiful and secluded as any in the southwest.

	Passage Cove SW 763,268	Durgan Beach SW 773,272	Grebe Beach SW 775,272	Porth Saxon & Porthallack SW 780,270 / SW 781,269
SUNBATHING	3	3	5	4
SECLUSION	2	2	3	3
SWIMMING	3	4	4	4
SAND	3	3	3	3
ROCKPOOLS & CAVES	3	3	2	3

SOUTH SHORE THE BEACHES

The estuary's southern beaches are all accessed via a secretive path that winds through woodland adjacent to the shore. The first – unnamed – beach is reached by walking down a slipway towards the water, then picking your way back along the seafront in the direction of the car park for around 200 metres. Another 10 minutes of walking along the original path will bring you to another unnamed – and very hidden – cove, which is accessed from a tiny track that leads off to your left. The woods open out at Bosahan Cove, where fine golden sand sweeps down to where waves swell at the shore. And, after around another 10 minutes of walking along the path, you will reach the peaceful and shaded Ponsence Cove, and its tiny neighbour that sits behind rocks to the left.

	Unnamed 1 SW 762,263	Unnamed 2 SW 769,264	Bosahan Cove SW 773,262	Ponsence Cove SW 777,261
SUNBATHING	2	4	5	5
SECLUSION	3	5	4	4
SWIMMING	4	4	5	4
SAND	3	4	5	3
ROCKPOOLS & CAVES	3	3	4	4

THE PITSTOPS

North Shore

Run by the upmarket Wright Brothers restaurant group, The Ferryboat Inn at Helford Passage is now as much of a must-visit stop for its food as it is for the views it offers over the water. Secure a table on its beachside terrace, and order a plate of oysters – reared just along the estuary at Porth Navas – before tucking into the likes of Fowey mussels, Cornish crab and pan-fried prawns.

The Ferryboat Inn, Helford Passage, TR11 5LB. 01326 250625. ferryboatcornwall.co.uk

South Shore

It might be slightly off-route, but The Shipwright Arms in Helford is worth the diversion. Just a few minutes' walk from the South Shore ferry slipway, it's a great place for a pint. The ubiquitous local Doom Bar bitter is here on draught, of course, but the Betty Stogs beer and bottled Helford Creek cider are equally tempting.

The Shipwright Arms, Helford, TR12 6JX. 01326 231235. shipwrighsthelford.co.uk

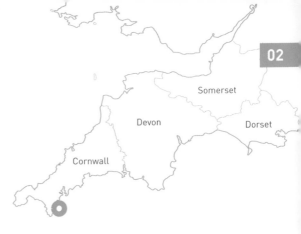

Somerset

Devon

Dorset

Cornwall

These two neighbouring beaches are among this corner of England's most secluded. Downas Cove, the more deserted of the two, is a narrow splatter of sand edged by glistening rocks, on which saltwater pools mix and swirl as they attempt to fight their way back to the sea. Lankidden, its larger sibling, offers a wide strip of pale-yellow that, at low tide, provides access to tiny satellite coves that are hidden away on either side. Both are perfect spots for wild swimming; gentle inclines on each allow you to ease yourself into the water gently, letting each wave-ripple accustom you further to bracing Atlantic temperatures. Our suggested walk is an incredibly simple one. The route takes you along the Coastal Path to Lankidden – where ropes are provided to help with the steep descent to the beach – and onto Downas.

| TR12 6SH | THE WALK 2km / 40mins | BEACH ACCESS | Lankidden SW 756,166 Downas SW 763,167 |

EBB & FLOW

Downas only reveals its sand for an hour or so either side of low tide. Lankidden is accessible until mid to high tide. Both beaches are inaccessible once the sea comes in. There is a large area of grassy headland above Downas Cove, which you can use till the water retreats.

THE PITSTOP

Perched on Dolor Point, looking back along the coastline towards Downas and Lankidden, The Paris Hotel may have an incongruous name, but in every other respect it's as Cornish as the blue-and-white pilchard boats that lie clumsily on the shore in front of its forecourt. Pints of Wreckers Ale and St Austell HSD are poured in the cosy bar area, while the Oceanview Restaurant offers a very affordable, daily changing menu dominated by fresh local seafood – think spiced haddock, baked pollock or a simple basket of battered cod and chips. It also serves up a range of vegetarian and vegan options, which isn't always a given in this part of the southwest.

The Paris Hotel, The Cove, Coverack, TR12 6SX. 01326 280258. pariscoverack.com

GETTING THERE

— Head south on the B3293. Turn right at Zoar Petrol Station after Goonhilly and follow signs to Ponsongath and Gwenter. After about a mile, turn right to Ponsongath. Turn left at the Methodist church and follow the road for one mile, then take the track on the right before the farm. Follow this right down to the bottom and park on the headland after the last gate. Parking costs £1 (payable in an honesty box).

1 Leave your car, walk out onto the grassy headland, then turn left and head eastwards along the Southwest Coastal Path.

2 After around 200 metres – just after you cross a stream and climb to the top of a dip – you will see the access path for Lankidden Cove on the right. The walk of 10 minutes or so gets incredibly steep towards the end, and you may want to make use of the rope banisters provided. Make sure they're securely attached before letting them take your weight.

3 To get to Downas Cove, head back to the Coastal Path and continue east for another 15 minutes. This will lead you into Downas Valley.

4 Go over two stiles and walk past a grassy area on the right. You can get onto the beach just after you cross the footbridge.

5 To return to the car park, simply head back along the Coastal Path.

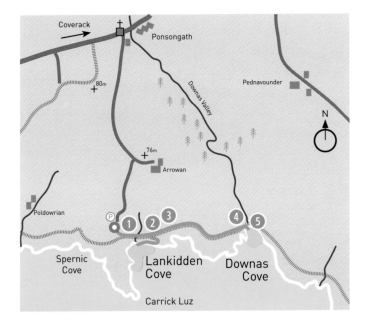

	Lankidden Cove	Downas Cove
SUNBATHING	4	5
SECLUSION	4	5
SWIMMING	4	4
SAND	5	5
ROCKPOOLS & CAVES	2	5

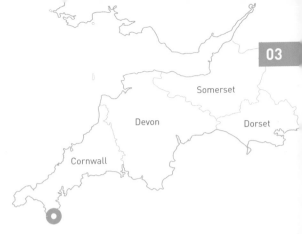

The walk we've suggested here, around the Lizard Point, is the longest in the book for good reason. The full 15-kilometre route takes you around the most southerly parts of the British mainland, and past Kynance Cove – one of Cornwall's most spectacular and popular coastal stretches. It's secret beaches we're concerned with, though, and Housel Cove and Pentreath Beach are stunning alternatives to the people-packed sands of their near-neighbour. At low tide, pretty Housel – located at the base of a steep valley – rolls out like a carpet towards the blue waters of the bay, while Pentreath rivals the famous surf spots of Fistral and Porthtowan in the amount of Atlantic swell that rears up before it. Don't let the length of our suggested walk put you off. The only hill worth worrying about is just after Church Cove at the beginning, and the rest of the route is as flat as can be. And, as you're never more than 20 minutes from your starting point in Lizard village, you're under no obligation to do the walk in its entirety. We seriously recommend you do though.

TR12 7NQ

THE WALK
15km
2hrs 30mins

BEACH
ACCESS

Housel
SW 708,119
Pentreath
SW 693,127

GETTING THERE

— Head south on the A3083 into Lizard village and park on the green in the centre.

1 From the car park, follow signs down the lane to Church Cove. Walk all the way down to the Coastal Path and turn right.

2 Follow the path for 45 minutes or so, past the lifeboat station and the Housel Bay Hotel.

3 When you reach the bottom of a steep valley, turn left and descend the steps to Housel Cove. To continue on to Pentreath Beach, carry on along the Coastal Path. This takes you past the lighthouse and, around 30 minutes later, to the tip of the Lizard – the most southerly point in mainland Britain. There's a café serving good cream teas here, and an honesty-box shop where you can pick up some jam for your own homemade version.

4 Continue along the path and, 50 minutes or so later, you will reach Pentreath Beach. At the time of writing, the steps down to the beach were closed because of erosion, but the local council have plans to fix this.

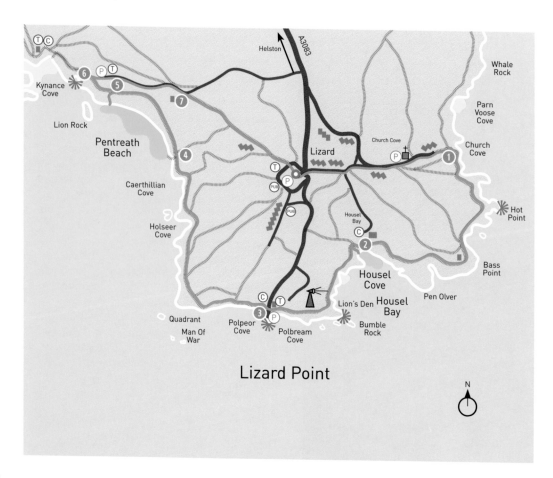

Lizard Point

5 If the steps are inaccessible, the only way down to the beach is via a steep and precarious path that threads through loose rock. You can find it on the far side of the beach as you walk along the Coastal Path. Take care if you do decide to go down – and make sure you're wearing suitable shoes.

6 To continue with our suggested route, return to the Coastal Path and carry on walking along. After around 10 minutes, you will see the beautiful Kynance Cove. To get down to it, take the access path that leads straight ahead.

7 To return to your car, head for the viewpoint above Kynance Cove then walk back through the car park behind you. Go up the lane and, at the first sharp bend around 400 metres in, turn onto the pathway that leads straight ahead into the fields. Follow this for 15 minutes or so back to Lizard village.

THE BEACHES

The first secret beach you'll come to on the walk is Housel Cove. A pretty inlet that looks out into Housel Bay, it is cloistered within a deep, south-facing valley, and protected from strong currents by the Bumble Rock and Pen Olver headlands on either side. Like most of the beaches on this section of coastline, its existence depends on the tides. But when the sea is out, the sands can spread into the bay for an impressive distance, making it an ideal spot for sunbathing and swimming.

Pentreath Beach, towards the end of our suggested walk, is a wide, flat sandy beach that is adored by in-the-know local surfers. They come because of the lack of submerged offshore rocks and its regular full-force pounding from the Atlantic Ocean. When the conditions are on the tranquil side, you can rely on Pentreath to be deserted. The perilous descent required deters all but the most adventurous of walkers.

	Housel Cove	Pentreath Beach
SUNBATHING	4	4
SECLUSION	3	4
SWIMMING	5	4
SAND	5	5
ROCKPOOLS & CAVES	4	4

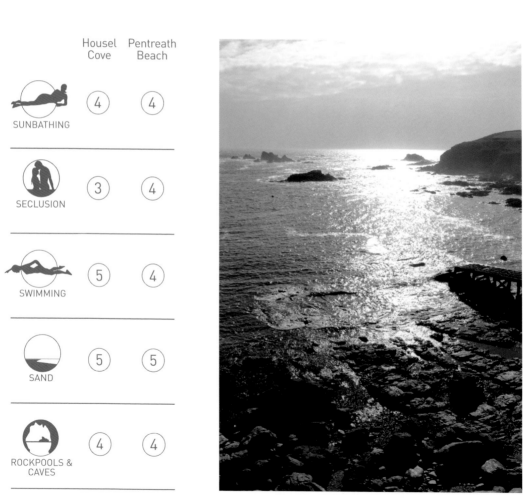

THE PITSTOPS

The most southerly village in mainland Britain, Lizard is a lively place that thrives on tourism, and caters well for the visitors that pass through it on the way to Lizard Point and Kynance Cove. It has two excellent pubs that specialise in freshly made, locally sourced food, and it's also home to several cafés, coffee shops, fish and chips takeaways, and lovely little restaurants. You can even pick up jams and pickles at The Most Southerly Honesty Box Shop, which also bizarrely sells a selection of chintzy jewellery. We've highlighted our favourites here – the two village pubs, mainland Britain's most southern café and a fine-dining hotel restaurant – but there are many others.

Buzzing gastropub The Witchball, situated between the village green and Lizard Point, is as popular with locals as it is with tourists. Parts of the building date from the 15th century, and its atmospheric black-and-white bar is a great place to sample the fine range of Cornish beers and ciders – many of which, including Witch Ball and Lizard Point, are supplied by the small, independent Organic Brewhouse. The restaurant is equally good. Fish and seafood are brought in daily by local fishermen, and everything from handmade pasties to vegetables are sourced from less than a mile away.

The Witchball, Lighthouse Road, Lizard, TR12 7NJ. 01326 290662. witchball.co.uk

The Top House Inn is a more traditional establishment, which serves all the usual St Austell ales – including Korev, its new Cornish lager – in a long, curved bar area. Its super-fresh seafood sets it apart, though. The crab and lobster are especially good as, each day, the man responsible for supplying them pops in to drop off his catch and have a pint of Doom Bar at the bar. He wouldn't be sticking around if he was ashamed of it, would he?

The Top House Inn, Lizard, TR12 7NQ. 01326 290974. thetophouselizard.co.uk

Looking down onto Polpeor Cove, Polpeor Café – also known as The Most Southerly Café – occupies one of the most desirable locations on the British coast. Its landmark status ensures a regular influx of visitors in all seasons, though its wonderful cream teas and all-day breakfasts would pull in punters even if it were located in a subterranean car park. As it's unlicensed, visitors are welcome to bring along their own drinks to accompany the food – which ensures that meals here remain very much in the budget category.

Polpeor Café, Lizard, TR12 7NU.
01326 290939

Set on a clifftop away from the village, Housel Bay Hotel may have a slightly Fawlty Towers feel, but there's nothing deranged about the welcome you'll receive here. And with talented chef Joe Roussel in the kitchen, Waldorf salads shouldn't be a problem. Sit in the floor-to-ceiling-windowed dining room and gaze out over the sea as you tuck into French-inspired dishes such as partridge with Madeira jelly or confit of duck with foie gras. The hotel also offers a bistro menu – grilled sardines, crab tart – at lunchtime, as well as sandwiches and cream teas.

Housel Bay Hotel, Lizard, TR12 7PG.
01326 290417. houselbay.com

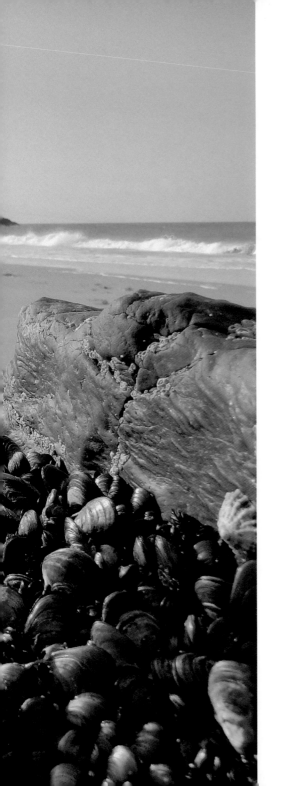

Somerset

Devon

Dorset

Cornwall

A mere 20-minute walk from the ever-popular Praa Sands, Rinsey Beach provides a wonderful alternative to the thronging shores of its near-neighbour and the other beaches of Mount's Bay. With one half comprised of soft, feet-tickling sand and the other of craggy, pool-concealing rocks, this cove is ideal for anyone looking to while away a warm, sunny day. And, though the tides have been known to deposit a fair amount of seaweed on its shore, it comes close to idyllic once it's all been washed away. Our suggested walk – a simple downhill stroll to the beach past an old tin mine – is one of the shortest in this book. But take care at the bottom of the access path; the steps have eroded and can get slippery.

| TR13 9TS | THE WALK 1km / 20mins | BEACH ACCESS | SW 593,269 |

THE PITSTOP

Though the interior – more youth club than cosy country inn – may disappoint after the promise of its white-and-black traditional exterior, The Lion & Lamb in Ashton makes a perfectly good pitstop on this section of the Coastal Path. Winner of the local council's Platinum Chefs' Award in 2015, it does pub grub very well indeed – and the excellent mixed grills, sirloin steaks, and portions of scampi and chips are accompanied on the menu by several good vegetarian and vegan options. If you're just here for a drink – perhaps in one of its two beer gardens – you can take your pick from the likes of Cornish Knocker, Betty Stogs and Spring Chicken, as well as all the usual suspects.

The Lion & Lamb, Fore Street, Ashton, TR13 9RW
01736 763227.

GETTING THERE

— Head east on the A394 from Penzance towards Helston and, just before Ashton, take the turning signposted Rinsey. Follow the road all the way down to the car park.

1 Exit the car park at the back and follow the track all the way down the hill.

2 When you reach the old tin-mine stack, look out for the beach-access path that leads off diagonally to the right. Follow this down to the sands.

3 To return, simply retrace your steps.

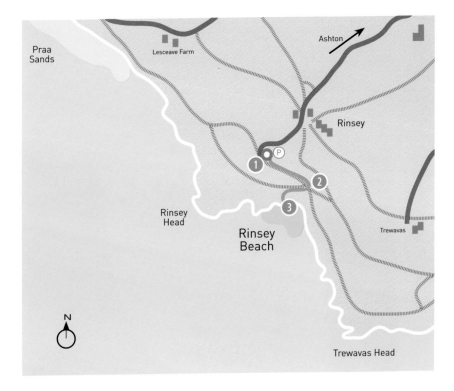

SUNBATHING

SECLUSION

SWIMMING

SAND

ROCKPOOLS & CAVES

EBB & FLOW

Rinsey Beach ceases to exist at high tide. But separate sandy and rocky areas are revealed when the sea goes out, making the beach ideal for both lounging and exploring.

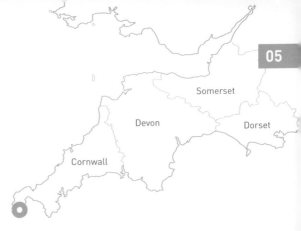

Somerset

Devon

Dorset

Cornwall

An idyllic half-moon of enticing yellow sand, Porth Chapel is the sort of secluded beach that anyone with a love of the sea goes to sleep dreaming about. Its setting is simply stunning, and the view from the shore incorporates the remains of an old chapel, a waterfall that pours down flower-flecked cliffs and the spire of St Levan church rising from the fields behind. Our suggested walk should last around an hour, but – what with stopping to admire the scenery – it may well take longer. The walk back inland from the beach, over streams and along grassy pathways, is particularly breathtaking.

TR19 6JR

THE WALK
3.5km / 1hr

BEACH
ACCESS

SW 381,218

EBB & FLOW

Porth Chapel offers a large area of flawless, large-grained sand to enjoy when the sea is out. And, though the beach area is significantly reduced by the incoming tide, the sand is still perfectly accessible.

THE PITSTOP

Close to the famous clifftop Minack Theatre, just along the coast from Porth Chapel, the Cable Station Inn at Porthcurno is popular with the pre- and post-show crowds in summer. It might not be the most attractive of pubs – though its flower-fringed outdoor terrace is perfectly pleasant – but there's usually a good atmosphere in its open-plan bar, as well as a fine selection of Sharp's Brewery ales and ciders. It serves decent pub grub all day, too. And if you're there on a warm evening, you might even find yourself getting involved in one of its legendary barbecues.

Cable Station Inn, Porthcurno, TR19 6JX
01736 810479. cablestationinn.co.uk

GETTING THERE

— Take the B3315 from Land's End in the direction of Penzance. Turn right in Polgigga and follow signs to Porthgwarra. Follow the road through the village to the car park. Charges vary, depending on the length of stay.

1 Exit the car park and follow the lane down to the beach. Find the tunnel on the left-hand side of the cove. Join the Coastal Path, which is signposted beside houses here.

2 When the path splits after 10 minutes or so, bear right and walk down to Porth Chapel. The beach is accessed via rocks that act as makeshift steps.

3 To continue on our suggested route, retrace your steps over a footbridge and take the path inland to the top of a small valley. After a couple of minutes, take the right-hand turning onto a path that leads to the other side.

4 Cross a stone footbridge and continue up the lane to St Levan church. Turn left and, after 50 metres, left again onto a lane that crosses a stream.

5 Walk up this lane, over a stile and into fields. Follow the left-hand edge of the first field and go over the stone steps into the next-door field after around 100 metres.

6 At the next step of stone steps, cut across the field to the left rather than going over them. Continue in this direction and join the track that leads to Roskestal Farm.

7 At the farm, turn left along the road and walk towards Porthgwarra. Take the lane that leads off a sharp right-hand turn, and continue on to the village and car park.

5
SUNBATHING

4
SECLUSION

5
SWIMMING

5
SAND

2
ROCKPOOLS & CAVES

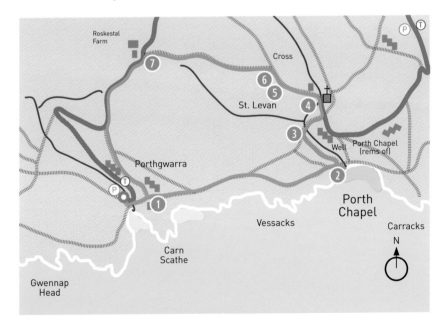

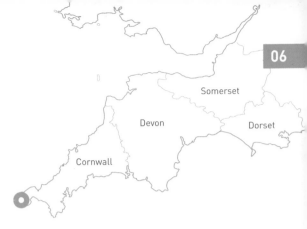

Somerset

Devon

Dorset

Cornwall

Home to the Song of the Sea, a tall, narrow natural arch that winks at the golden sand, Nanjizal is thought by many to be the finest beach on the Penwith peninsula. It's truly secluded, though; and often deserted. This may be down to its distance from any road or car park. But it's well worth making the effort to walk to, if only to check out its famous slit-like arch and some remarkable natural stone sculptures, including the Diamond Horse – an equine-shaped formation through which sunlight shines with a jewel-like glint. Caves and anenome-studded rockpools emerge when the sea retreats, and there's even a freshwater waterfall, which is ideal for washing off all that post-swim salt. Our suggested walk is a straightforward stroll through fields and farmland, which takes in a short section of the Coastal Path before emerging onto the beach.

TR19 7AQ

THE WALK
3.5km / 1hr

BEACH
ACCESS

SW 357,236

THE PITSTOP

Formerly the Little Barn Café, the Apple Tree Community Café & Art Studios opened its doors to the public as recently as May 2011. Situated in an old, tin-roofed barn in Sennen, the café lives up to its boho name with a lovely, light, green-and-white interior, in which bunting drapes from the beams, original artworks hang on the walls and the day's specials are chalked up on black-boards. It might not pour pints, but it serves up as much tea, coffee and soft drinks as you can handle, and its breakfasts and light lunches are as lovingly created as the décor. Make sure you try the delicious homemade cakes.

The Apple Tree Community Café & Art Studios, Trevescan, Sennen, TR19 7AQ.
01736 872753. theappletreecafe.co.uk

GETTING THERE

— Head down the B3315 towards Land's End and stop in Trevescan. Park your car in one of the laybys that are situated on either side of the village, around 200 metres away.

1 From either layby, walk into Trevescan village. Just opposite the bus stop, you'll see a footpath sign that points down a driveway. Follow this past two cottages (don't worry – it's a public right of way).

2 Take the path that leads into the fields and through Trevilley Farm. After you've passed through some more fields, bushes start to close up around the path. Keep following it around to the right (don't take the left turn) and walk along the valley-ridge.

3 At the point you first see the sea, take the path that leads downhill.

4 Go over a footbridge and down a set of wooden steps to the beach.

5 To return, simply retrace your steps.

SUNBATHING

SECLUSION

SWIMMING

SAND

ROCKPOOLS & CAVES

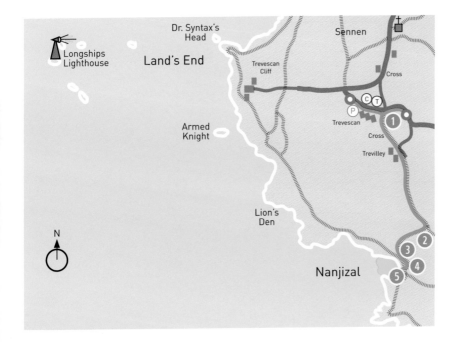

EBB & FLOW

Low tide brings large sandy areas, as well as caves and rockpools to explore. At certain times of year, particularly after big storms, the Atlantic strips Nanjizal's beach, revealing the rocks beneath. If the beach is inaccessible, use the grassy headland next to the waterfall till the tide goes out.

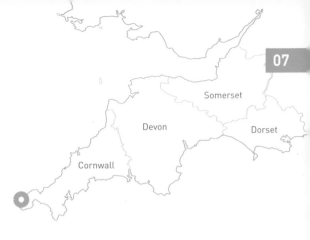

Somerset

Devon

Dorset

Cornwall

A wide slice of golden sand that has plenty of places to sit or stroll even at high tide, Gwynver makes a peaceful alternative to next-door Sennen Cove. Just across the water from Land's End, it offers stunning views of its noisy neighbour and Longships Lighthouse over Whitesand Bay. And though the full force of the Atlantic hammering on its shore attracts in-the-know surfers on high-season weekends, you'll have it pretty much to yourself the rest of the time. It's certainly isolated. Even getting to the nearest shop and toilet requires waiting for low tide and then walking across the sands to Sennen.

TR19 7BB

THE WALK
1.2km / 20mins

BEACH
ACCESS

SW 362,275

THE PITSTOP

The Old Success Inn, just five minutes' drive away from Gwynver at Sennen Cove, may have outgrown its 17th-century fishermen's pub origins – it is now home to a restaurant, 12 bedrooms and a self-catering apartment, as well as a bar – but it's still a great place for a drink. The views from the pub over the churning sea and wide sweep of sand are rarely less than spectacular, and the Cornish hand-pulled ales – which include St Austell Tribute and Proper Job – are superb. Food doesn't stray too far from the pub grub formula, but when the location is this good, who cares?

The Old Success Inn, Sennen Cove, TR19 7DG
01736 871232. oldsuccess.co.uk

GETTING THERE

— Take the A30 towards Land's End. Then on a left-hand bend, just after the junction with the B3306, take the small road on the right. Bear right when the road splits after 100 metres or so, and keep going until you see signs for a car park. Parking costs £2.

1 From the top car park, follow the path that begins opposite the layby on the road. This leads down steep steps for around 10 minutes to Gwynver.

2 If you're beginning the walk in the lower car park, you can join the path at the point where it runs adjacent to the bench and picnic table.

3 Once you've reached the beach, you can return via the same steps. Be warned: as it's more than a 70-metre ascent from the shoreline to the car park, this can be hard-going.

SUNBATHING 5

SECLUSION 3

SWIMMING 4

SAND 4

ROCKPOOLS & CAVES 2

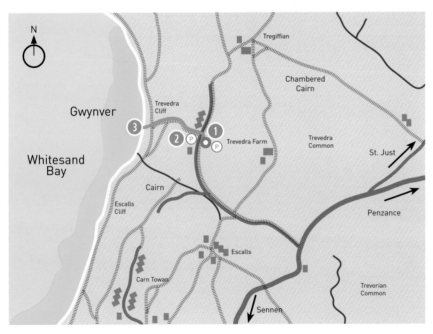

EBB & FLOW

There's plenty of sand exposed at low tide, which enables you to walk all the way over to Sennen Cove. And though the Atlantic has been known to submerge Gwynver at very high tide, a large sandy area usually remains.

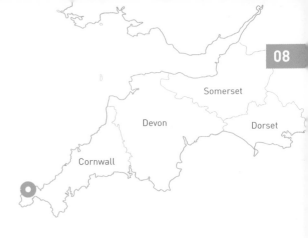

Somerset

Devon

Dorset

Cornwall

Situated between Pendeen and Morvah Points, Portheras Cove is one of Cornwall's best-kept secrets. Its beige-coloured, bucket-shaped sweep of sand has escaped the popularity of its neighbours due to its relative inaccessibility and the fact that it has only been open to the public since 2004 – when the clean-up operation after a ship ran aground here in the 1960s was finally completed. Our suggested walk takes you to the coastline via fields and farmland in which the ghostly remnants of shrub-shrouded tin mines poke through the landscape. And, with only one steep headland to negotiate, it's ideal for families.

TR19 7TU

THE WALK
3.5km / 45mins

BEACH
ACCESS

SW 388,357

EBB & FLOW

Though severe tides and storms can carve Portheras Cove's soft sand away, making it slope steeply down to the sea, there's always a sizeable sandy area at low tide. Only a tiny section of the beach remains when the sea comes in, but you can wait on the grassy headlands above till the water retreats.

THE PITSTOP

Part of the Schoolhouse Arts & Community Centre, Morvah's Gallery Coffee Shop provides beach visitors with the opportunity to combine scones with sculpture and buns with brushstrokes. Open from 10.30am to 5pm in the summer months, it serves hot drinks, delicious homemade cakes and cream teas in a refreshingly informal setting, in which jam-scoopers sit surrounded by a ramshackle selection of frames and canvases. It's also been known to host the occasional jazz evening.

The Gallery Coffee Shop, The Schoolhouse Arts & Community Centre, Morvah, TR20 8YT
01736 787808. morvah.com

GETTING THERE

— Head west on the B3306 from St Ives and, around 200 metres after Morvah, take the right-hand turning to Chypraze Farm. Follow this all the way to the parking area operated by the farm. Parking costs £2 – there is an honesty box just outside the farmhouse.

❶ When you come out of the car park, head towards the farm and take the left-hand track after the first building on the left.

❷ Turn left onto another path just before the track ends. You will see the turn for the Coastal Path after a couple of minutes. Do not go down it for now.

❸ Follow the original path over stepping stones and across a stream down to the beach.

❹ To continue with our suggested walk, return to the path and go left at the Coastal Path turning. Follow the track up and over the headland, past several derelict tin mines.

❺ At the crossways, after around 15 minutes, turn right to Morvah. The village is 500 metres ahead.

❻ Turn right at the road beside the church. The Gallery Coffee Shop is 50 metres or so further on.

❼ After the coffee shop, turn right onto the B3306 and, after 50 metres, go over the steps opposite the postbox. Make your way across the fields to the road that leads back to Chypraze Farm and your car.

SUNBATHING

SECLUSION

SWIMMING

SAND

ROCKPOOLS & CAVES

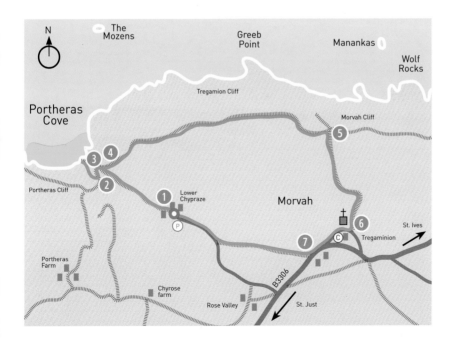

Somerset

Devon

Dorset

Cornwall

Designated a Site of Special Scientific Interest due to its rare rock striations and exposed granite cupola, Porthmeor Cove is renowned for being one of the southwest's most important geological destinations. Rocks certainly feature heavily, and the beach has a wonderfully echoey, ends-of-the-earth feel that's reminiscent of the basalt beaches around Northern Ireland's Giant's Causeway. As there's no car park close to the cove, our suggested walk is a long one. It takes in the rugged beauty of Gurnard's Head and Porthmeor Point, as well as dramatic views of Pendeen Lighthouse and an ancient menhir. The wide, sheltered beach is roughly halfway along the route, so there's plenty of opportunity to stretch your legs as you make your way there and back.

TR26 3DE

THE WALK
5km
1hr 15mins

BEACH
ACCESS

SW 425,374

EBB & FLOW

Many large rocks and rockpools are exposed when the tide is out. And there are some great wild swimming opportunities off Porthmeor Point to the right. At high tide, the beach is almost completely covered, though the headland has several flat, grassy areas on which you can sit till the sea retreats.

THE PITSTOP

Owned and run by chef Charles Inkin – who had food critics in raptures with his previous venture the Felin Fach Griffin in Wales – and overseen by head chef Bruce Rennie, formerly of Michelin-starred restaurant Shanks in Belfast, the Gurnard's Head is head and shoulders above most pints-and-pilchards Cornish inns. People drive for miles to sample its ever-changing seasonal menus, and anyone venturing down to Porthmeor Cove should definitely allow time to stop here and tuck into dishes such as spider crab tagliatelle and seabass with braised fennel. But you'll be equally well served if you just want to drop in for a pint. Make sure you try the Skreach dry cider, brewed on a tiny scale in nearby St Buryan.

The Gurnard's Head, near Zennor, TR26 3DE
01736 796928. gurnardshead.co.uk

GETTING THERE

— Travel west on the B3306 from St Ives, and park your car at the Gurnard's Head pub, which is situated on a sharp bend just before Porthmeor. There is also a car park on the verge here.

1 Follow the road from the pub into Treen village. When the road comes to an end, take the path on the left down to the Coastal Path. As you approach the headland, you will need to take the right-hand fork when the path splits.

2 At the crossways, go left along the Coastal Path towards the beach. If you'd like to enjoy some particularly stunning views, you could opt to go straight ahead at this point and take a short detour around Gurnard's Head.

3 Cross a footbridge and walk up to a small headland. You will find the access path to the beach at the front of this.

4 To continue with our suggested route, carry on along the Coastal Path for a short distance, then turn left onto a track that follows a stream into the valley.

5 Once you've passed an old chimney stack, take the footpath on the left signposted Treen. Follow this through the hamlet of Lower Porthmeor and into a field.

6 Go through the farmyard ahead of you, and over a stile into a field that contains a standing stone.

7 Join the B3306 on the other side of this field, and walk the short distance back to the Gurnard's Head pub and your car.

SUNBATHING

SECLUSION

SWIMMING

SAND

ROCKPOOLS & CAVES

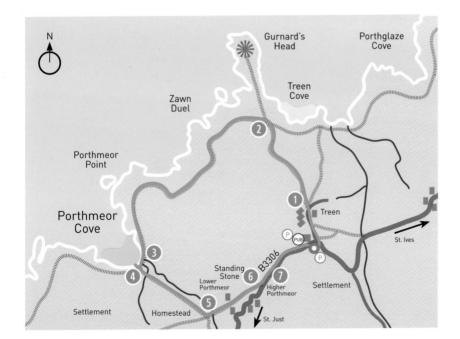

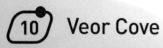

10 Veor Cove

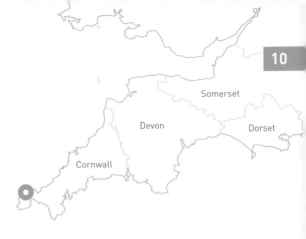

Somerset

Devon

Dorset

Cornwall

Usually deserted, even in high season, Veor Cove is a favourite of both wild swimmers and naturists – though, as it requires a strenuous and sometimes tricky walk to get there, neither comes that often. Were it easier to reach, the beach would no doubt be packed. Its pancake-flat, pale-yellow sand, which leads into sheltered, glass-clear water is, after all, ideal for all types of bathing. There are some lovely, creature-packed rockpools on either side of the sandy crescent, and the cliff-flanked channel that leads out to sea positively invites you to float through on your back, and look up through rocks to clouds and seabirds above. Our suggested walk takes in some wonderful coastal and moorland views.

| TR26 3BY | THE WALK
5.5km
1hr 15mins | BEACH
ACCESS | SW 445,388 |

EBB & FLOW

The sand takes on a half-moon aspect at low tide, and leads on to some excellent swimming opportunities around Carnelloe Long Rock on the left. When the sea comes in, the beach is submerged, though the rocks at the back remain accessible. Relax on the flat areas of the headland until the tide goes out.

THE PITSTOP

Serving breakfast, light lunches, and superlative cream teas, Heather's Coffee Shop is located on the scenic road that gently winds along the coast of Land's End from St. Ives to Penzance (B3306). This is the top spot to order a hearty and healthy fry up before you head off on a long walk or the place to refuel between secret beach hunting trips with a slice of their most indulgent cake. Situated in an Area of Outstanding Natural Beauty and walking distance from a couple of world heritage status local attractions (Geevor Tin Mine Museum, Levant Mine), plus other interesting landmarks such as Pendeen Lighthouse and Tregeseal Stone Circle, this is a popular stop-off with locals who are always happy to give you tips about what to do in the area.

Heather's Coffee Shop, 11 Church Road, Pendeen, TR19 7SF. 01736 788069

GETTING THERE

— Head west along the B3306 from St Ives, and take the turning to Zennor on your right. The car park is situated just behind the Tinners Arms pub. Parking costs £3.

❶ Go through the gate in the far right-hand corner of the parking area and turn left onto the lane. After 10 minutes or so, this turns into a pathway.

❷ Turn left almost immediately onto the Coastal Path. Follow this down into a valley.

❸ Go down some steps, over a footbridge and past Pendour Cove. On a bend, about 50 metres on from a bench, you will see an offshoot track that leads to Veor Cove.

❹ Once you've visited the beach, you can either retrace your steps back to Zennor or take our suggested circular route by continuing along the Coastal Path from the point at which it meets the beach-access track.

❺ Round the headland on the other side of Veor Cove and, when you see Gurnard's Head come into view, take the path that leads around the back of the house on the left.

❻ Once you've passed the house, go down the driveway track until it meets a lane. Turn left here, then, just before the lane joins the road, turn left again and cross over a small bridge.

❼ On the first left-hand bend in the lane, take the path to the right and follow it through the fields all the way back to Zennor.

SUNBATHING

SECLUSION

SWIMMING

SAND

ROCKPOOLS & CAVES

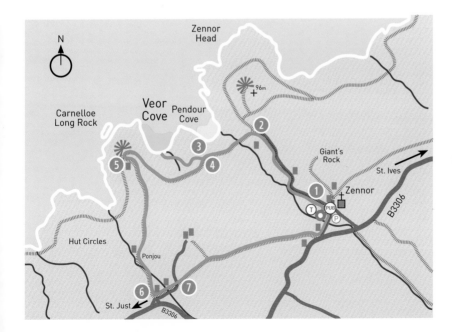

North
Cornwall

North Cornwall

		Page
⑪	Fishing Cove	66
⑫	Porth Joke	70
⑬	Diggory's Island Sand	74
⑭	Fox Cove	78
⑮	The Shifting Sands of Doom Bar	82
⑯	Tregardock Beach	90
⑰	Benoath Cove	94
⑱	The Strangles	98
⑲	Stanbury Mouth	102

Trevos
Head

St. Ives
Bay

St. Ives

Camborne

Atlantic
Ocean

Bude Bay

● Bude

Holsworthy ●

⑲

⑱

Tintagel
Head

⑰

Tintagel ●

⑯

Launceston ●

Pentire
Point

⑮

Trevose
Head

⑭

Wadebridge ●

⑬

Bodmin ●

Liskeard ●

⑫

Cornwall

Newquay ●

Lostwithiel ●

St. Austell ●

St. Agnes

Gribbin
Head

Truro ●

English
Channel

Dodman
Point

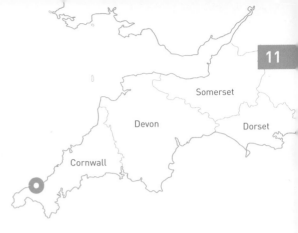

Somerset

Devon

Dorset

Cornwall

Though it's just a few hundred metres from a car park, Fishing Cove is as secluded a beach as any in the book – as the naturists and skinny-dippers to be found strolling its soft, golden shore on sunny afternoons and evenings would no doubt testify. The reason behind its secretiveness is one of geography. The access path down to the beach is steep and as slippery as the seals that often swim up to bask on the sand – and it isn't one you should attempt if you're at all afraid of heights. Our suggested walk is a simple one, but it's not for the faint-hearted.

TR27 5EG

THE WALK
1.5km / 20mins

BEACH
ACCESS

SW 595,428

THE PITSTOP

A proper, family-run village pub, the Red River Inn in Gwithian is just a short drive from Fishing Cove. Its Biblical-sounding name comes from the ruddy iron ore that used to run down local rivers from the tin mines at Redruth and Camborne, and its somewhat austere exterior has changed little from the days when thirsty workers from those pits would bang tankards on its wooden door. Inside, though, it's a relaxing space of cream walls and pale wood-panelling. Renowned for serving a great, regularly changing selection of Cornish ales, it also dishes up solid pub fare of the scampi, chips and rack of ribs variety. Keep an eye on the specials board – the chef often chalks up fresh local fish or other seasonal produce.

Red River Inn, Prosper Hill, Gwithian, TR27 5BW.
01736 753223. red-river-inn.com

GETTING THERE

— Head north out of Hayle on the B3301, and follow the road through Gwithian and past the turning for Godrevy car park. You will see another free car park at the top of the hill, just before the Hell's Mouth Café. Leave your vehicle here.

1 Exit the car park at the end and join the Coastal Path. Follow the path for 300 metres or so.

2 Turn right down the narrow beach-access pathway. Watch your footing as you descend to Fishing Cove.

3 To return, simply retrace your steps.

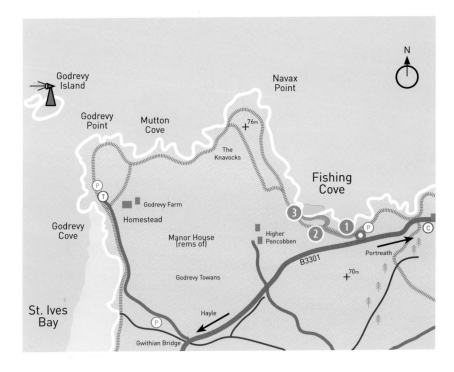

5
SUNBATHING

5
SECLUSION

5
SWIMMING

5
SAND

3
ROCKPOOLS & CAVES

EBB & FLOW

At low water, the beach slopes gently into the sea, making it ideal for swimming – especially as the water is protected from currents by Navax Point. At high tide, the sea comes up to the cliff, but a small area of beach is still accessible.

Somerset

Devon

Dorset

Cornwall

Porth Joke – known locally as Polly Joke – is a long, wide, unspoilt beach that burrows deep into green, craggy hills between Pentire Point West and Kelsey Head. Its large expanse of sand means it's ideal for those looking for a leisurely day of lounging, while its proximity to the surf resorts of the North Cornish coast means it gets a board-worthy battering from the Atlantic waves, too. There are plenty of secluded nooks and crannies to be found here, though its most secret spot emerges at mid to low tide, when a swim around rocks leads to a truly cut-off space in which the outside world seemingly ceases to exist. Our suggested walk leads around Pentire Point West, and offers fabulous views over Crantock Beach and the River Gannel estuary.

TR8 5SE	THE WALK	BEACH	SW 772,605
	2.5km / 30mins	ACCESS	

EBB & FLOW

The sheer depth of the beach means
that plenty of sandy areas remain
accessible in all but the highest of tides.
To take full advantage of its attractions,
though, visit at mid to low tide.

THE PITSTOP

Set on a headland, looking down on the wide,
golden sands of Crantock Beach, The Bowgie
Inn is an attractive, slate-roofed building that
seems to have outgrown its pub origins and
become something of a low-key entertainment
complex. It has three bars – the oak-beamed
Pigsty, surf-themed Ocean and more classic
Conservatory – as well as an outdoor terrace
and beer garden. And though the eclectic menu
on offer throughout (which offers everything
from homemade steak-and-kidney pie to
cheese-and-pineapple toasties) can sometimes
seem as bewildering and sprawling as the
venue itself, there's a laid-back sense of fun to
it all. And you can't argue with the views.

The Bowgie Inn, West Pentire, Crantock,
TR8 5SE. 01637 830363. bowgie.com

GETTING THERE

— From the A30, travel north on the B3075 and, just before Newquay, turn left to Crantock and West Pentire. Follow the road all the way to West Pentire and leave your vehicle in the car park. Charges vary, depending on the length of stay.

1 Come out of the car park and turn right down the road you came in on. Take the first turning on the left.

2 Go through the kissing gate and, 100 metres or so further on, turn left onto the Coastal Path.

3 Follow the path over a footbridge and on the right you will see the short beach-access path.

4 To visit the super-secluded part of Porth Joke, walk through the field that runs along the headland on the far side of the beach.

5 As you near the front of the headland, you will see a hillock, behind which you'll find some rocks that you can scramble down to get to the sand.

6 To continue with our suggested route, cross back over the footbridge and, after 50 metres or so, take the path on your left. Follow this for 20 minutes around Pentire Point West.

7 When the path splits, turn right towards West Pentire village and return to the path you set out on. This will lead back to your car.

SUNBATHING

SECLUSION

SWIMMING

SAND

ROCKPOOLS & CAVES

Somerset

Devon

Dorset

Cornwall

A wonderfully secluded corner of the spectacular yet popular Bedruthan Steps, Diggory's Island Sand is only accessible from the beach at very low tide. To visit its deep arc of pale-gold sand at any other time requires following our suggested walk around rugged Park Head, and watching your footing as you edge your way down to the deep-blue lagoons that collect around its shoreline. Don't forget your swimming trunks. No matter how low the water temperature is, you're going to want to jump in and splash around.

PL27 7UU

THE WALK
3.5km / 1hr

BEACH
ACCESS

SW 848,703

EBB & FLOW

This beach has a very slight gradient and the sea retreats by around 150 metres at low tide. When the water starts coming in, it offers plenty of swimming opportunities around the small islands and outcrops.

THE PITSTOP

Just a wave-splash from the sea on Mawgan Porth bay, The Merrymoor Inn may have a somewhat functional 1930s exterior, but indoors it is as warm and friendly as any centuries-old Cornish tavern. As it's a freehouse, the selection of beers and ciders is extensive and varied, and can feature anything from Dartmoor Cornish Legend to St Austell Proper Job. And the large food menu includes the likes of stone-baked pizzas and fresh local seafood alongside all the usual pub grub suspects. It does get very busy with tourists in the summer months, though, and in high season you can pretty much forget about securing a place on the outdoor terrace.

The Merrymoor Inn, Mawgan Porth, TR8 4BA
01637 860258. merrymoorinn.com

GETTING THERE

— Head north out of Mawgan Porth on the B3276, and drive past the two car parks that serve the Bedruthan Steps. Continue along the flat road and, just as you start to go downhill, look out for Park Head car park, which displays a National Trust sign. Park your vehicle here for free.

1 Walk out of the other end of the car park from the one you came in on and head left along a path that takes you through fields.

2 Turn left at the signpost, and follow the path all the way down to the coast.

3 Look out for the access path to the beach on your left. This leads you down the sloping headland for around 100 metres to some precarious-looking rocks, which you must scramble down to get to the sand.

4 To continue with our suggested route, climb back up to the path and head left. Follow the network of paths that hug the cliff-edge, and look down on the coves and lagoons that emerge between the jagged rocks and islands.

5 Continue around the headland until the paths merge to descend into Porth Mear. You can swim out to explore the islets and sea caves from this point.

6 To carry on towards the car park, take the path on the right before the footbridge. This leads you through a conservation area into a field. Head uphill here and around the back of a farmhouse.

7 Turn left along the lane, and you will arrive back at your car in a few moments.

SUNBATHING

SECLUSION

SWIMMING

SAND

ROCKPOOLS & CAVES

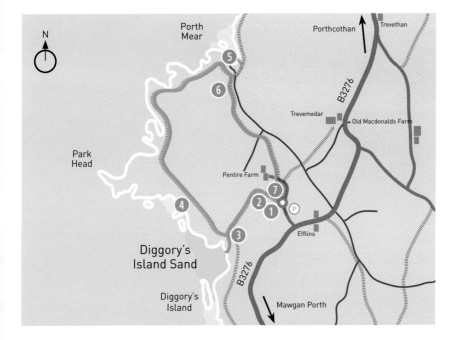

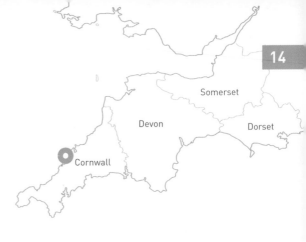

Somerset

Devon

Dorset

Cornwall

A wide crescent of sand, spliced in two by a mussel-crusted spike of rock, Fox Cove is the largest of the three inlets that sit between Treyarnon Bay and Porthcothan. Completely inaccessible at high tide, the beach reveals its smooth, butter-yellow sweep when the water retreats, and the deserted shore presents a glorious alternative to all the sun-seeking and sandcastle-digging going on at neighbouring Porthcothan. Our suggested walk takes you along a gently undulating clifftop path and past the wave-pounded Minnows Islands. The only challenge arises on the final part of the descent to the beach. Watch your footing.

| PL28 8LW | THE WALK 5km 1hr 15mins | BEACH ACCESS | SW 855,733 |

THE PITSTOP

A hangout for the area's many surfers and musicians, The Tredrea Inn at Porthcothan has built up an enviable reputation as a live-music venue over the years. A drink or two there in the evening – accompanied by the sound of any number of local bands – can be a lot of fun, but things are much, much quieter in the daytime. Though, at first glance, the pub doesn't seem to have much to get excited about, it's a perfectly pleasant place in which to nurse a pint of St Austell Tribute or Doom Bar, or tuck into a plate of more-than-decent pub grub. And the views from the garden over Porthcothan Bay are wonderful.

The Tredrea Inn, Porthcothan, near Padstow, PL28 8LN. 01841 520276

GETTING THERE

— Take the B3276 south from St Merryn and, when you arrive in Porthcothan, park in the council car park. Charges vary, depending on the length of stay.

1 Turn right on the road outside the car park. You'll see Porthcothan Beach immediately on your left. To get to Fox Cove, cross the bridge and take the track on the left.

2 Walk for 50 metres or so up the headland and join the Coastal Path on the right. At the crossways, go straight ahead. This track will take you north along the cliffs, and past Minnows Islands.

3 After walking for around 25 minutes, you will arrive at the area behind Fox Cove, which is home to an RSPB reserve and a campsite. The access path down to the beach is on the far side, on the left near a bench.

4 When the path splits halfway down, take the left-hand fork. This precarious route winds down to some rocks. Scramble over these to the sand. Take care.

5 To return to your car, simply retrace your steps.

SUNBATHING

SECLUSION

SWIMMING

SAND

ROCKPOOLS & CAVES

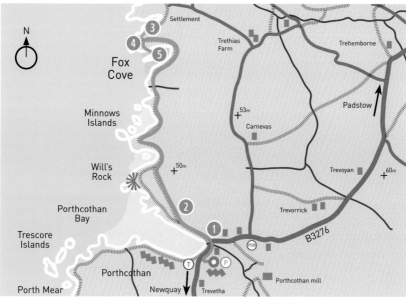

EBB & FLOW

This beach is something of a paddling pool at low tide – and with a bit of a scramble, you can get out to the rock in the bay for a spot of jumping and diving. The access path begins halfway up the beach, so be careful not to get cut off when the tide comes in.

15 The Shifting Sands of Doom Bar

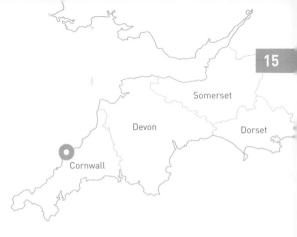

Somerset

Devon

Dorset

Cornwall

The shoreline of the River Camel estuary is popular for good reason. Whether people come to surf at Polzeath, where Atlantic swell is refined and concentrated by Pentire and Stepper Points on either side of the bay, or to relax in the fashionable restaurants and deli-cafés of Rock and Padstow, they all come home raving about the area's raw beauty. Much of this is due to the sand. A result of tidal and geological swirling over centuries, the soft golden powder that coats the estuary and piles up in the bays and inlets at low tide may look stunning, but it's not known as Doom Bar for nothing. Many a ship – more than 600 in the past 200 years – has foundered on the bars and strands in Padstow Bay, and it's reputed sailors would rather sit out a storm at sea than attempt to shelter here. Our suggested short walk along the northwestern edge of the bay takes in two beautiful beaches, Hawker's and Harbour Cove, as well as many views worth getting your camera out for.

PL28 8HR

THE WALK
2.5km / 45mins

BEACH
ACCESS

Hawker's
SW912,775
Harbour
SW911,769

83

HAWKER'S COVE

Little more than an inlet from which
fishing boats set out into the bay,
Hawker's Cove is a gorgeous slice of
pastel-coloured sand, bordered by
rockpools that line its edges like ink-
splats. The walk along the shore in
either direction from here offers near-
perfect views over the water.

EBB & FLOW

At low tide, there's a sizeable area of
sand that leads out to the notorious
Doom Bar in the estuary. And the inlet
close to the slipway is well sheltered
from the wind. The sea covers the
whole area at high tide so, at this time,
it's best to head on to Harbour Cove.

HARBOUR COVE

This wide strip of soft sand makes an ideal base for a day on the Doom Bar. Situated just five minutes from the car park, it gives onto secluded, rock-fringed sand slips at its edges that dissolve into the water of the estuary.

EBB & FLOW

Enormous at low tide, Harbour Cove still offers a large strip of sand when the sea comes in. It's a beach that you can visit at any time of day.

THE PITSTOP

Starting point of the world-famous 'Obby 'Oss celebrations – in which men dressed as horses dance around the village on May Day, pretending to catch the local girls – The Golden Lion Hotel is the oldest pub in Padstow. Its flower-hung, whitewashed exterior gives onto two lovely, traditional bar areas in which open fires crackle and blaze. It would be perverse to come here and not have a pint of Doom Bar when you're so close to the eponymous sands, but the pub also serves Cornish Coaster and several other local beers and ciders. Food-wise, it's very good indeed. All meat comes from local butchers Button Meats, and the small selection of homecooked meals – including an excellent steak and chips – err towards the hearty rather than the healthy.

The Golden Lion Hotel, Lanadwell Street, Padstow, PL28 8AN. 01841 532797. goldenlionpadstow.co.uk

GETTING THERE

— Head north on the B3276 out of St Merryn and, just before you reach Padstow, take the left turn signposted Crugmeer and Hawker's Cove. Follow the road for around 10 minutes, until you see signs for the car park just before Lellizzick. Costs vary, depending on the time of year. The car park is closed in winter.

1 Exit the car park at the bottom and take the track that leads directly downhill to Harbour Cove.

2 To carry on to Hawker's Cove, either follow the Coastal Path north or simply walk along the sand.

3 To continue with our suggested circular route, take the small lane at the back of Hawker's Cove and follow it all the way back to your car, just after Lellizzick.

4 For an optional extra walk after leaving Hawker's Cove, continue on the Coastal Path around Stepper Point, passing the lookout station – a distance of around 1.5 kilometres. To return, simply follow the path back to where you started.

	Harbour Cove	Hawker's Cove
SUNBATHING	5	2
SECLUSION	3	1
SWIMMING	2	2
SAND	5	2
ROCKPOOLS & CAVES	4	4

[Map showing: N, Stepper Point, Broadagogue Cove, Greenaway Beach, Trebetherick, Lookout Station, 74m, Pepper Hole, Padstow Bay, Butter Hole, Lellizzick, Hawker's Cove, Daymer Bay, P, Padstow, The Doom Bar, Harbour Cove, Brea Hill 62m]

Somerset

Devon

Dorset

Cornwall

It only takes a few minutes of wandering along the wild, west-facing Tregardock Beach for you to realise it takes a regular pounding from Atlantic storms. The headland looks as though it's on the verge of collapse, caves and overhangs have been smashed out of the base of the cliffs, and juggernaut-sized boulders lie tossed around the stream-crossed, golden sand as though they're mere pebbles. Even the mussels and barnacles that cling to the rocks seem to have a grim determination to their grip. Our suggested walk takes in several steep ascents before leading you back along winding paths through some of Cornwall's most beautiful countryside.

PL34 0HB

THE WALK
10km / 2hrs

BEACH
ACCESS

SX 040,841

EBB & FLOW

This beach is best at mid to low tide – and you should take care when the sea starts coming back in. The water returns at an angle, so the access steps are cut off before the rest of the beach. If you're swimming, be careful of rip tides.

THE PITSTOP

Though The Port William (theportwilliam. co.uk) at Trebarwith Strand is a very fine pub, which offers food and beer that are every bit as good as the coastal views from its lovely sun terrace, the most charming spot close to Tregardock Beach has to be The Strand Café. Situated just a few metres from the stunning beach at Trebarwith Strand, it serves up a selection of sandwiches, burgers and salads, as well as delicious homemade cakes to a distinctly windblown clientele. The walls of the tiny building act as an exhibition space for local artists – many of whom are regulars – and the vibe is relaxed and informal. It's a wonderful place in which to hang out or even to just pick up a takeout coffee.

The Strand Café, Trebarwith Strand, PL34 0HB
01840 770276. thestrandcafe.co.uk

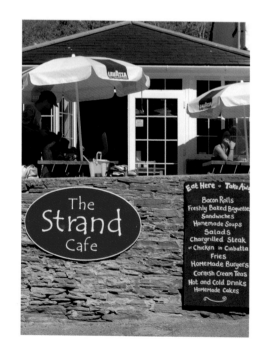

GETTING THERE

- Drive south from Bude on the A39. Just after Starapark, turn right onto the B3314 and, shortly after passing through Slaughter Bridge, take the right-hand turn onto the B3263. Turn left towards Trebarwith Strand after a couple of kilometres and follow the road all the way down to the car park.

1. Walk towards Trebarwith Strand beach. Take the lane up to the pub and turn left, then go through the car park and over a stile, and turn right onto the Coastal Path.

2. Walk up and over the headland. Continue along the path for around 20–25 minutes and turn right at the crossways. This path leads you down to Tregardock Beach.

3. To continue with our suggested route, return to the crossways and go straight ahead. As you near Tregonnick Farm, turn left onto the path that leads across the fields.

4. Bear right in Treligga village, then turn left and left again down a dead-end road.

5. Go through a gate and past farm buildings before rejoining the path by another gate on the right. Walk along the left-hand edge of the field and through another field. As you approach Trecarne Farm, walk across to the coastal side of the buildings and through the gate next to a telegraph pole.

6. Walk up the concrete farm road for 50 metres, then turn left onto the path after the farmhouse.

7. Follow this to Besloe. Turn left at the road and walk along for 300 metres before turning left onto the footpath at Trebarwith village. Follow this all the way to Trebarwith Strand, turning right at the crossways.

SUNBATHING 4

SECLUSION 4

SWIMMING 2

SAND 5

ROCKPOOLS & CAVES 5

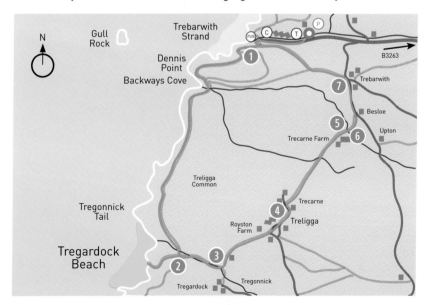

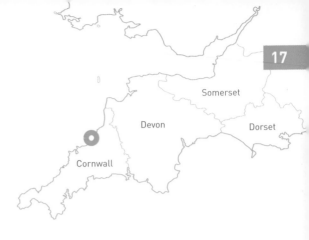

Somerset

Devon

Dorset

Cornwall

Burrowed into the wild North Cornish coastline, Benoath Cove is a truly spectacular beach. Its fine golden sand is ideal for sunbathing, its relatively sheltered waters perfect for wild swimming, and its rockpools and six caves – one of which passes right through the cliff – are sure to appeal to anyone with an adventurous spirit. Our suggested figure-of-eight walk takes in the best of the coastline around Tintagel, supposedly once home to King Arthur and the Knights of the Round Table, and leads you around Barras Nose and Tintagel Head to Merlin's Cave. Even without any wizarding associations, it would still be utterly magical.

PL34 0AY

THE WALK
6km
1hr 30mins

BEACH
ACCESS

SX 068,893

EBB & FLOW

There's a large area of soft sand to enjoy at low tide, as well as access to all the cave mouths. The only drawback is that when the sea is out, the beach is accessible on foot from busy, next-door Bossiney Haven. Benoath Cove is almost completely submerged at high tide.

THE PITSTOP

In a village that buzzes with tales of swords being pulled from stones and ladies emerging out of lakes, you can't blame a pub for cashing in on Arthurian legend. Thankfully, the King Arthur's Arms Inn in Tintagel alludes to the village's favourite castle-dweller only in name, and what could have been a touristy tavern of round tables and Camelot cocktails is actually a pleasantly traditional stone-walled Cornish inn with a good selection of local ales and ciders. Though the menu sticks fairly rigidly to British pub favourites – steak-and-kidney pie; gammon, egg and chips; bangers and mash – the meat is generally locally sourced, and the menu large enough to suit even the most discerning tastes.

King Arthur's Arms Inn, Fore Street, Tintagel, PL34 0DA. 01840 770628. kingarthursarms.co.uk

GETTING THERE

— Head south to Bossiney on the B3263 from Boscastle. Once you're in the village, follow signs to the car park.

❶ Take the path down to Bossiney Haven beach. Bear right when you enter the field and walk towards the headland.

❷ Turn left onto the Coastal Path and then right onto an offshoot path that leads all the way down to the beach. There are steps and ropes to help you down.

❸ To continue with our suggested route, go back up to the Coastal Path and turn right. Follow it for five minutes, then go down some steps and straight over at the crossways.

❹ Should you wish to return to Bossiney early, you can take the path that leads diagonally off to your left after 15 minutes. It's just before you enter a small, grassy vale.

❺ To carry on, walk around the front of Smith's Cliff to Tintagel Head. You'll find toilets, a shop and a tearoom here. Climb down to Tintagel Haven Beach to visit Merlin's Cave or cross the perilous bridge to check out The Island.

❻ Follow the track up to Tintagel village, and go left onto the road. When it bends to the left after the shops, continue straight ahead down the path into the fields.

❼ You will join the Coastal Path in the small, grassy vale you passed through earlier. Turn right up the path to Bossiney here. Go through a gate and up a pathway between the fields. When you reach the B3263 in Bossiney, turn left to return to your car.

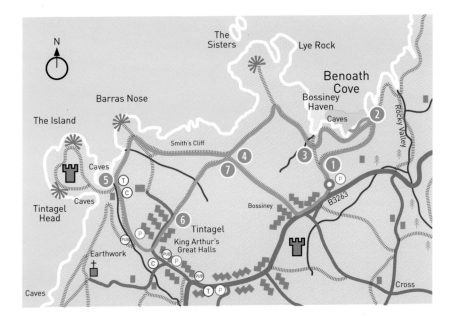

4

SUNBATHING

3

SECLUSION

5

SWIMMING

5

SAND

5

ROCKPOOLS & CAVES

Somerset

Devon

Dorset

Cornwall

A large stretch of sand and shingle, The Strangles remains quiet and little-visited even at the highest point of high season, due to the steep descent required to access it. Indeed, it's so secluded that parts of it have reputedly been used to shoot films of a – ahem – romantic nature. The beach rewards those who undertake the perilous descent, though. Backdropped by the kind of lead-grey, teeth-like crags that are so typical of North Cornwall, it is an atmospheric spot onto which the Atlantic Ocean relentlessly rolls rather than smashes. Pick an area of sand on which to lie, and let the gentle sound of waves lull you off to sleep. Our long suggested walk takes you over a high headland to the beach, and back through the sort of woodland you thought only existed in fairytales.

EX23 0LG

THE WALK
8.5km
2hrs 30mins

BEACH
ACCESS

SX 130,954

EBB & FLOW

This is a large, sandy beach at low tide, with plenty of rockpools and boulders to explore. But when the sea comes in, just a thin, pebbly strip remains. If you're swimming, be careful of rip tides.

THE PITSTOP

Situated on the Coastal Path, overlooking the beach at Crackington Haven, the Coombe Barton Inn wears its maritime heart on its sleeve – it even has a blue-and-white boat propped up against the wall outside. The décor inside may be a little on the tired side – parts of it have the feel of a church meeting hall – but you can't argue with the views from the outdoor terrace, or the selection of Cornish ales on draught. Meals, made with local ingredients, are homely and unpretentious, and a standard pub grub menu – fish and chips, mixed grill, breaded plaice – is supplemented by a regularly changing specials board that's dominated by fresh Cornish seafood.

The Coombe Barton Inn, Crackington Haven, EX23 0JG. 01840 230345. coombebarton.co.uk

GETTING THERE

— Head south on the A39 from Bude and, when you reach Wainhouse Corner, turn right towards St Gennys and Crackington. Drive along this road and follow signs to Crackington Haven. Once you've arrived in the village, leave your car in the car park. Charges vary, depending on the length of your stay.

1 Exit the car park, walk down to Crackington Haven beach and join the Coastal Path on its left-hand side. Head south along this path for around 45 minutes until you reach the marker post at the back of The Strangles.

2 When the path forks here, bear right and, after 100 metres or so, turn right again onto the beach-access path.

3 To continue with our suggested route, return to the marker post and take the path to Trevigue.

4 Turn left when you meet the road and walk along for around 100 metres. Take the second turning into a driveway, and enter a field through a gate on the left-hand side of the buildings.

5 Walk down to the bottom of the valley and into the woods. Turn left onto the path just before the stream and follow it along through the woods. Keep on the path till it crosses two footbridges in quick succession. You will exit the woods shortly afterwards and the path becomes a narrow lane.

6 Follow this all the way down into Crackington Haven.

SUNBATHING

SECLUSION

SWIMMING

SAND

ROCKPOOLS & CAVES

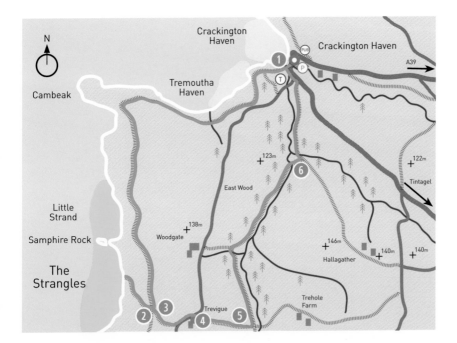

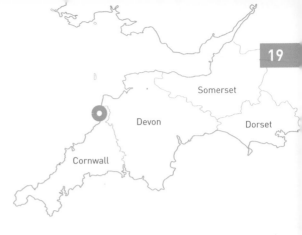

Somerset

Devon

Dorset

Cornwall

Popular with intrepid surfers, who come to ride the ferocious Atlantic waves that pound at its shores, Stanbury Mouth illustrates just how quickly the British coastline can change shape. When we started putting this book together, it was a fairly accessible – albeit very secluded – cove. Now, erosion has taken its toll on the access track, and getting down to the beach requires following a perilous path created by a stream that tumbles down the cliffside. This just adds to its air of secretiveness though. Indeed, it's so off the beaten track that locals claim a pack of feral dogs have made their home on the headland above. Our suggested walk is a short, undemanding gallop along the Coastal Path, with a steep climb to and from the beach.

EX23 9JQ

THE WALK
2.5km / 45mins

BEACH
ACCESS

SS 199,133

THE PITSTOP

Situated on the Coastal Path between Bude and Hartland, and a mere five-minute drive from Stanbury Mouth, The Bush Inn at Morwenstow is an atmospheric 13th-century inn that offers stunning views over the Atlantic coast. Its excellent selection of local beers includes smooth Skinners Cornish lager and the deliciously hoppy Keltek Magik, and it also has a fine range of wines and freshly pressed fruit concoctions – try the elderflower pressé, made with foraged ingredients. The food menu is made up of upmarket pub grub – steak and chips, beer-battered fish, beef casserole with dumplings – and the dessert list is longer than the mains. Good coffee, too.

The Bush Inn, Morwenstow, EX23 9SR.
01288 331242. bushinnmorwenstow.com

GETTING THERE

— Head north out of Kilkhampton on the A39 and, just before Crimp, turn left to Shop and Morwenstow. Drive through Shop and follow signs to Woodford. The lane becomes a farm road and, 500 metres further on, you will see a car park. Leave your vehicle in the second section.

1 Exit the car park on the farm track that runs between fields ahead of you. Follow this to the headland.

2 Turn left onto the Coastal Path and follow it down into the valley.

3 Take the path on the right that leads you down to a stream. From here, you can negotiate your way to the beach by clambering over rocks.

4 To continue with our suggested route, return to the path and follow it inland.

5 After 10 minutes or so, turn left up a track that leads you back to the car park.

SUNBATHING 3

SECLUSION 5

SWIMMING 4

SAND 4

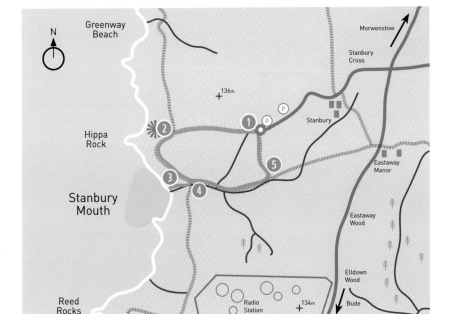

ROCKPOOLS & CAVES 3

EBB & FLOW

Large areas of rock-ringed golden sand are exposed at low tide, which provide an excellent launch point for surfing and swimming. When the sea comes in, the sandy areas disappear and the beach is comprised solely of large pebbles.

North Devon

North Devon

		Page
⑳	Welcombe & Marsland Mouths	110
㉑	Berry Beach	114
㉒	Mouthmill Beach	118
㉓	Rockham Beach	122
㉔	Lee Bay	126
㉕	Wild Pear Beach	130
㉖	Woody Bay	134
㉗	Wringcliff Bay	138

Morte
Point

Baggy
Point

Braunton

Atlantic
Ocean

Barnstaple Bay

Hartland
Point

Bideford

Hartland

Bradworthy

Bude

Foreland
Point

Heddon's
Mouth

㉖ ㉗

㉕

● Lynton

● Combe Martin

Exmoor
National
Park

● Barnstaple

● South Molton

Dulverton
●

● Atherington

Devon

Great Torrington

● Chumleigh

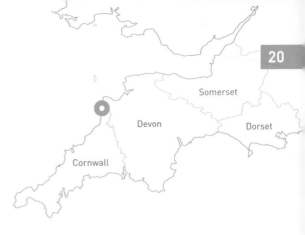

Somerset

Devon

Dorset

Cornwall

There's something almost architectural about Welcombe Mouth, which sits on the right-hand side of the Devon-Cornwall border. Tramlines of grey rock run in perfect symmetry down to the sea, and provide the beach with an industrial, semi-futuristic ambience. A favourite of surfers and wild campers, it can have a bit of a laid-back, party atmosphere at times – especially in and around the car park. By contrast, craggy Marsland Mouth, just over the headland, is as tranquil as they come. It makes perfect sense that the late poet and playwright Ronald Duncan's hut is situated here, and that he took daily inspiration from this wave-battered landscape. Our long suggested walk takes you into both Devon and Cornwall, through nature reserves and woodland, and onto a wonderful pub

EX39 6HL

THE WALK
7km / 2hrs

BEACH
ACCESS

Welcombe
SS 212,179
Marsland
SS 211,174

EBB & FLOW

At low tide, Welcombe Mouth is divided into areas of soft sand and rockpools. There's not as much sand at Marsland. Both beaches shrink at high tide, but the headlands above each are flat and grassy, and there are small rivers to swim in. Plus, there's a large, natural pool between the two waterfalls.

THE PITSTOP

Friendly and informal, The Old Smithy Inn in Darracott village may be thatched and traditional on the outside but, indoors, it exudes a design-savvy edge that wouldn't look out of place in a Shoreditch shebeen. Gloriously mismatched pieces of statement furniture sit against stylish swathes of bold-print wallpaper, and pillars are just as likely to be hung with Sixties and Seventies memorabilia as they are with old-fashioned horse brasses. The frequently changing menu makes good use of local produce – Bideford Bay squid, Clovelly cod and Spanish-style seabass ceviche all make regular appearances – and the bar serves up a good selection of Cornish and Devonian ales and ciders.

The Old Smithy Inn, Welcombe, Bideford, EX39 6HG. 01288 331305. theoldsmithyinn.co.uk

GETTING THERE

- Head north out of Kilkhampton on the A39. Just after the turning to Morwenstow, take the left-hand turn to Welcombe. Follow signs first to Mead then to Welcombe Mouth. The entrance to the car park is at the bottom of a very steep narrow lane.

1. Welcombe Mouth beach is directly in front of the car park. To continue to Marsland Mouth, turn left onto the Coastal Path and walk over the headland.
2. Descend into the valley and you will see the access path for Marsland Mouth beach on your right.
3. To continue with our suggested route, return to the Coastal Path and head left over the footbridge into Cornwall. Leave the Coastal Path after 100 metres and follow the path up the valley until it meets a track. Turn left and walk down into the valley and over a footbridge.
4. Around 150 metres after the footbridge, turn onto the right-hand path that runs into Marsland Wood.
5. Turn right when you reach a driveway, then go left onto a lane/track that leads uphill to Darracott.
6. Turn right onto a lane just after the farm buildings. The Old Smithy Inn is 200 metres further on, on the junction.
7. Go left at this junction and, after two minutes, turn left onto a track signposted Witheford. This becomes a path.
8. Walk through the fields until you reach Mead. Turn left onto the lane then, after 50 metres, right onto a track. This takes you through more fields to the headland.
9. Turn right here to return to the car park.

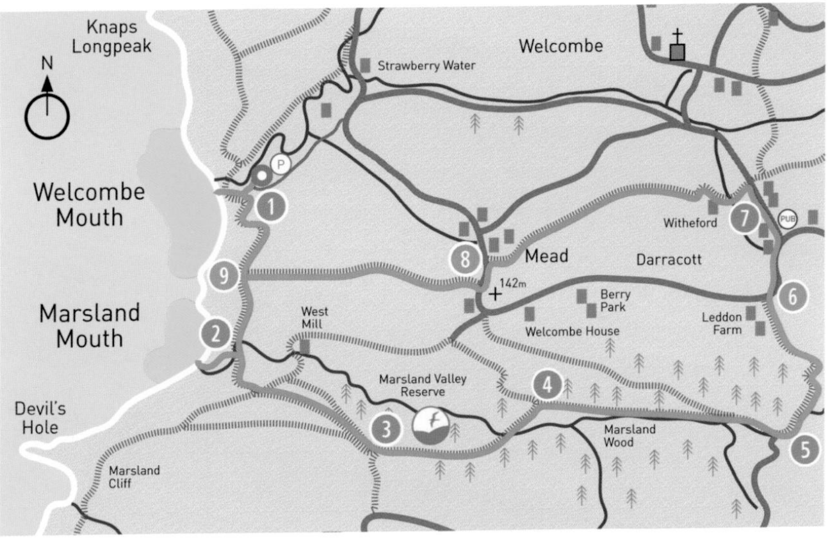

3 SUNBATHING

3 SECLUSION

4 SWIMMING

3 SAND

5 ROCKPOOLS & CAVES

Somerset

Devon

Dorset

Cornwall

Ideal for clambering and wild swimming, Berry Beach is sheltered by rocky fingers that stretch from the cliffs and reach out into the sea to act as natural breakwaters. The beach they protect combines areas of sand and rock to startling effect and, at low tide, it's perfect for bathing. There's even a waterfall close to the access path so you can wash off the saltwater on your return to shore. Our fairly long suggested walk takes you from pretty Hartland Quay to the ruins of an ancient abbey and along a river to the Coastal Path. Make sure you pause to take in the views as you walk along.

EX39 6DB   THE WALK   BEACH   SS 225,259
              5.5km   ACCESS
              1hr 30mins

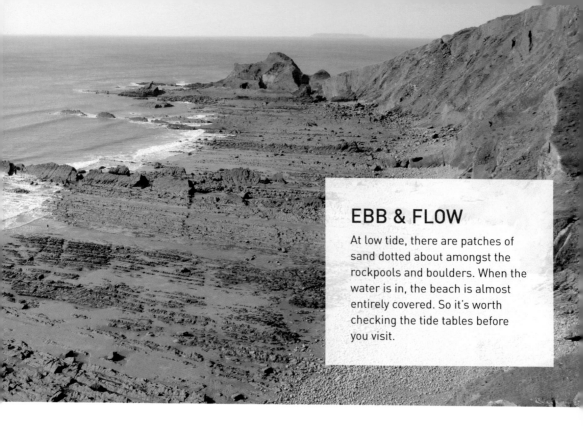

EBB & FLOW

At low tide, there are patches of sand dotted about amongst the rockpools and boulders. When the water is in, the beach is almost entirely covered. So it's worth checking the tide tables before you visit.

THE PITSTOP

Situated in the old stables of the Hartland Quay Hotel, the Wreckers Retreat Bar is a cosy, intimate place to stop for a pint at the end of your walk back from Berry Beach. The wood-panelled décor may be more Swiss chalet than traditional coastal inn – though it does display some slightly macabre relics from the ships wrecked on these shores alongside a selection of plastic fish – but you can't complain about the selection of beers from the nearby St Austell brewery or the sea views from its outdoor area. The food menu usually includes at least one dish made with fish plucked out of the Atlantic that day.

The Wreckers Retreat Bar, Hartland Quay Hotel, Hartland, EX39 6DU. 01237 441218. hartlandquayhotel.co.uk

GETTING THERE

— Head south out of Bideford on the A39 then, just after the Clovelly roundabout, turn right for Hartland and Lighthouse. Take this road and follow signs to Hartland. Once you're in the town, follow signs to Hartford Quay. Leave your vehicle in the top car park. Charges vary, depending on the length of stay.

SUNBATHING

1 Walk up and out of the car park, and onto the pathway that runs alongside the road.

2 Follow this past the coastguard's cottages, through the cemetery and, when you reach the end of the path at a lane in Stoke, turn left and walk down the hill.

SECLUSION

3 When the lane bends sharply, turn left onto a track and at the river, after 50 metres, turn left again onto a pathway that runs alongside the water down the valley.

SWIMMING

4 At the end of the path, cross the stone bridge into a field and follow signs to the Coastal Path. Walk past Blackpool Mill and over the headland.

5 When you reach the bottom of the next valley, turn left onto the beach-access path.

SAND

6 To return, simply follow the signs to Hartland Quay on the Coastal Path. You will be retracing your steps as far as Blackpool Mill, then climbing one more hill and crossing the headland over to the car park.

ROCKPOOLS & CAVES

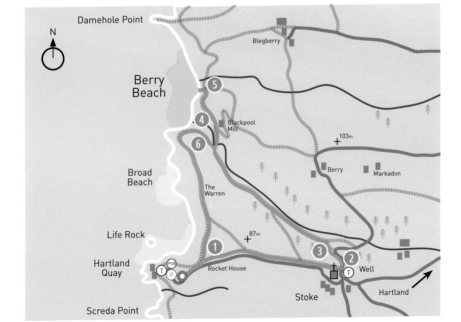

Somerset

Devon

Dorset

Cornwall

22

This is a beach of contrasts. A stream idly trickles through football-sized boulders down to the sea, while soothing sweeps of light-brown sand provide a backdrop to jutting rock formations that point arrow-like towards the Atlantic. It's a place for exploring rather than lounging, though flat grassy areas above the sea wall are ideal for reclining on while you listen to the babble of water below. Our suggested walk, over several wooden footbridges and onto a headland that affords some gorgeous coastal views, is one of the prettiest in this book. Lovely all year round, it's particularly beautiful in spring when bluebells line the woodland paths.

EX39 6AP	THE WALK 4km 1hr 15mins	BEACH ACCESS	SS 297,265

EBB & FLOW

The boulders exposed at low tide may be impossible to lie on, but there are patches of sand closer to the sea. When the tide comes in, the beach is almost entirely submerged. However, you can still enjoy the views from the sea wall.

THE PITSTOP

Brownsham, which consists of little more than a cowshed and a chicken coup, doesn't have a pub, so you'll need to either come prepared with a packed lunch or venture elsewhere for refreshment after your walk. In either case, we recommend The Point café, located between the Hartland Point Lighthouse and Lundy Heliport. Serving a hearty mix of paninis, pasties and rolls, as well as a variety of tasty cakes and locally roasted coffee, it caters well for walkers, who often describe it as 'a mirage on the coastal path'. You can call in advance to order a pre-packed lunch and, if it's tipping down by the time you get here, they'll even bring a warming mug of hot chocolate to your car. Closed November to Easter.

The Point @ Hartland, Hartland Point, Hartland, EX39 6AU. 07977 010 463. thepointhartland.co.uk

GETTING THERE

— Head south out of Bideford on the A39 and, just after the Clovelly roundabout, take the right turn on the bend, signposted Hartland and Lighthouse. Turn right at the first turning to the lighthouse. Turn right twice more and you will arrive at Brownsham car park.

1. Come out of the car park on the far left and take the path that leads towards the woods. Go through the gate and into the trees, taking the path on your right.
2. Follow this path for five minutes or so, then turn left onto a path that takes you down to a stream. Cross the footbridge, then turn right.
3. After another five minutes of walking, take the right-hand fork of the path downhill to the Coastal Path.
4. Turn right onto the Coastal Path and follow it over the headland. Just after you exit another wood, turn left onto a track. This will take you down to Mouthmill Beach.
5. To continue with our suggested route, take the track from the beach up through Brownsham Wood, passing the track you came down on. When this joins another track, bear right, keeping the stream on your left.
6. Continue along this track, and turn right onto another track at the top of the hill.
7. Walk through Lower Brownsham Farm, turn left onto a lane and then right into the car park.

SUNBATHING 2

SECLUSION 5

SWIMMING 3

SAND 1

ROCKPOOLS & CAVES 5

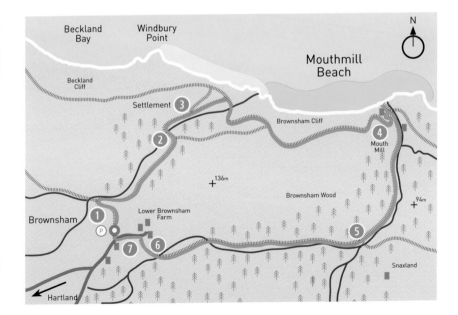

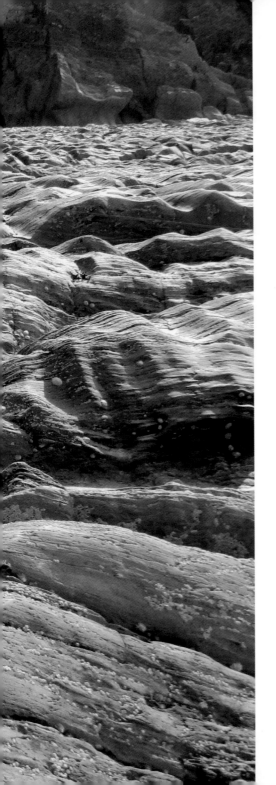

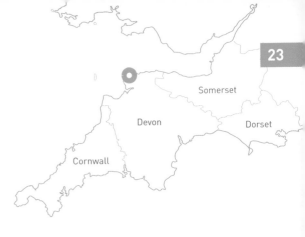

Somerset

Devon

Dorset

Cornwall

One of the larger beaches in this book, Rockham gets relatively busy on summer weekends but, even in high season, there's always a soft patch of sand available from which you can watch the waves and soak up the sun. To the left, there are angular rows of rocks, serrated like a kitchen knife, and dozens of rockpools in which you can forage for your supper. The rest of the beach is given over to flat, rock-dotted sand. Our suggested walk out to Morte Point is a long one, though we've provided several shortcuts should your legs start to tire. Wild swimmers should be careful of the currents around here – the local pub isn't called The Ship Aground for nothing.

EX34 7DR

THE WALK
5.5km
1hr 10mins

BEACH
ACCESS

SS 458,460

THE PITSTOP

Named after the many vessels that have foundered on the rocks around Morte Point, The Ship Aground is the busiest and best of Mortehoe's three pubs. An attractive, traditional white inn, built on the village's sloping main square, it pulls in the punters with a good selection of local beers and a fabulous fresh fish specials board that includes everything from plaice and hake to shark and lobster. Its cosy, low-beamed bar plays host to an open-mic session on Friday nights, which might appeal if you fancy belting out a sea shanty or two on your way back from Rockham Beach. If not, you can always relax with a pint of Doom Bar in the pub's lovely garden.

The Ship Aground, Mortehoe, EX34 7DT.
01271 870856. shipaground.co.uk

GETTING THERE

— Head north out of Woolacombe on the well-signposted seafront road and follow it along the headland into Mortehoe. Drive through the village until you see the car park on your right.

1 Leave the car park and walk along the lane situated opposite its entrance.

2 After five minutes or so, turn left up the pathway signposted Rockham Beach.

3 Continue on this path, and it will take you all the way to the beach-access steps.

4 To continue with our suggested route, climb back up the steps and turn right onto the Coastal Path. Follow it along the cliffs to Morte Point (look out for the shortcut paths off to the left, which lead back to the village).

5 Carry on along the Coastal Path, which will eventually return you to Mortehoe village – make sure you take the left-hand fork as you near the road. Walk past the old chapel and the church, and you will see The Ship Aground pub on your left. The car park is just a little further on from here.

SUNBATHING

SECLUSION

SWIMMING

SAND

ROCKPOOLS & CAVES

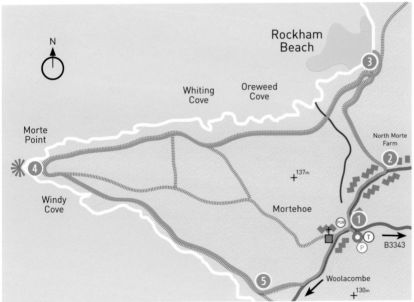

EBB & FLOW

The sea retreats a long way at low tide, revealing hundreds of rockpools. It also leaves a large area of sand and small, polished pebbles. There's hardly any beach left when the sea comes in, but the headland behind has plenty of flat grassy areas from where you can enjoy the views.

Somerset

Devon

Dorset

Cornwall

A beach of three parts – each smaller and more secluded than the last – Lee Bay is easily accessed from the road, and is backdropped by a selection of charming seafront cottages. The first section once acted as the village harbour, and it's still possible to see ancient slipways gliding over the rocks into the sheltered waters of the bay. The second, reached through a fissure in the rock, and over stepping stones and steps worn smooth by generations of fishing folk, is made up of polished, sun-warmed pebbles that are as comfortable to lie on as any sand. The final part can be reached by walking over protruding, dog-teeth rock shards, which give onto a seldom-visited cove that exists only at the whim of the tides. Our suggested walk takes you to all three, as well as through the woodland that lies behind, and on to the village pub.

| EX34 8LR | THE WALK
3km / 45mins | BEACH
ACCESS | SS 476,467 |

THE PITSTOP

Nobody – even the current owners – seems
to know why the sign at The Grampus Inn,
situated at the heart of Lee village, shows an
orca. Not that it matters. You're guaranteed
to have a whale of a time should you choose
to stop at this 14th-century pub. Its excellent
menu includes veggie options such as
mushroom and chestnut casserole and stir-
fried Asian greens alongside the usual bangers
and mash-type selection, and Newmans Red
Castle Cream or Exmoor Beast are available
to take into its lovely, flower-filled garden. It's
worth visiting for the cream teas served in the
garden alone.

The Grampus Inn, Lee, EX34 8LR.
01271 862906. thegrampus-inn.co.uk

GETTING THERE

— Lee Bay is relatively difficult to find without a good map. Drive west out of Ilfracombe on the A399 and, as you are leaving the town, take the turning on your right signposted Lee. Follow the road for around 10 minutes and, when you reach the seafront, park your vehicle in the car park on the left.

1 Walk out of the car park and down onto the main section of beach.

2 To get to the second section, go through the fissure in the cliffs directly ahead of you as you look toward the sea.

3 Reach the final and most secluded part by walking round the rocks that are closest to the water on the far side of the beach.

4 To continue with our suggested route, return to the second section of beach and climb the steps up the cliff. Follow the pathway that goes left at the top.

5 Continue along this path – don't be tempted to turn off when it joins two other tracks – until you reach a lane. Turn right here.

6 Walk along this lane for five minutes or so and, when you reach the second sharp bend, take the path that leads off to the left. This will take you through fields into a wood.

7 Follow the path downhill through woodland, and cross a footbridge and stile into a field.

8 Join the path on the other side of the field. Turn right for The Grampus Inn or left for the car park.

SUNBATHING

SECLUSION

SWIMMING

SAND

ROCKPOOLS & CAVES

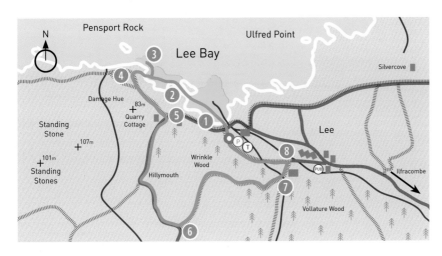

EBB & FLOW

The largest section offers an expanse of grey, tiddlywinks-like pebbles at low tide, which lead down to water sheltered from currents and rip tides. The second and third parts are only accessible when the sea is out. The main beach, in front of the village, is completely submerged at high tide.

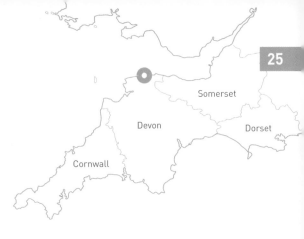

Somerset

Devon

Dorset

Cornwall

Just around the corner from the busy and popular Combe Martin, Wild Pear Beach is a favourite of local naturists – though its name, we promise, is not some weak, *Carry On*-style pun. The nudists come for the absolute seclusion that the beach offers and, as a sign on the way down points out, you mustn't be shocked to see naked flesh against the backdrop of sandy flats and steep, plant-hanging cliffs. Our short but challenging suggested walk takes you along some stunning, hilly sections of the Coastal Path, before winding back inland through scenic farmland and flower-fringed lanes. Clothing, you'll be glad to hear, is perfectly acceptable.

| EX34 0DN | THE WALK 3km / 1hr | BEACH ACCESS | SS 581,477 |

THE PITSTOP

A perfect spot from which to watch the sunset after walking back from Wild Pear Beach, the apostrophe-heavy Fo'c's'le Inn resembles a giant sugarcube looming over the thronging sands at Combe Martin. Its large terrace looks over the harbour and across the craggy bays and cliffs to the west, and – in summer – is usually full of high-spirited drinkers, quaffing pints of Exmoor Ale or any of its three guest bitters. The menu sticks to reassuring English pub fare, though it occasionally throws in some inspired fresh fish dishes if the local boats have brought in anything to pique the chef's interest.

The Fo'c's'le Inn, Seaside, Combe Martin, EX34 0DJ. 01271 883354. focsleinn.co.uk

GETTING THERE

Head north on the A39 and the A399 from Barnstaple and drive into Combe Martin. Follow signs to the seafront car park called 'Kilv'. Charges vary, depending on the length of your stay.

1 Exit the car park at the rear and walk uphill, following signs to the Coastal Path.

2 Follow the path up and over the headland, adjacent to Wild Pear Beach. You will be able to get a good aerial view of where you are headed from this point.

3 After 15 minutes or so of walking, you will pass a footpath leading off to the right signposted Combe Martin. Go down the left-hand path by the bench 50 metres further on. This will take you all the way down to the beach.

4 To continue with our suggested route, return to the Combe Martin path and follow it through fields until it joins a track that leads off to the right. Go down here and cross over a small bridge.

5 When this track becomes a lane, walk for another 50 metres or so and turn onto the path on the right. This takes you all the way to Combe Martin.

6 When you meet the main road, turn right and walk along it to the car park.

SUNBATHING 4

SECLUSION 5

SWIMMING 4

SAND 4

ROCKPOOLS & CAVES 3

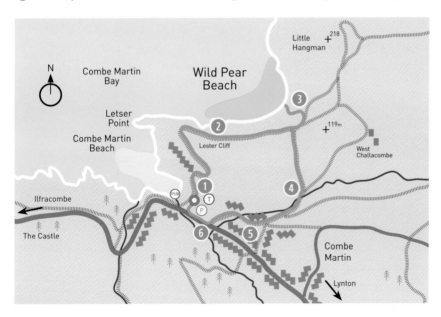

EBB & FLOW

This is a large beach, and you will have no problem finding an ultra-private spot at low tide. Though the beach shrinks when the sea comes in, an area is still useable as the access path joins the sand at its highest point.

Somerset

Devon

Dorset

Cornwall

The cliffs along the Exmoor coastline, particularly those east of Lynmouth, are among the highest in the country. And this can lead to some long and arduous descents to its beaches. This is certainly true of Woody Bay, though this stunning stretch of shoreline more than compensates for any aching shins. The aptly named beach is gorgeous at every level – densely wooded hills plummet down to huge rock buttresses, flat sandy plains and, finally, the Atlantic, and the views are exceptional. Our suggested walk follows a leafy lane through picture-postcard cottages, and past moss-bordered waterfalls and ancient bridges down to the sea.

EX31 4QU

THE WALK
2.5km / 45mins

BEACH
ACCESS

SS 677,489

THE PITSTOP

It might be a little out of your way, but it's well worth driving for a few minutes to visit The Hunter's Inn in the nearby Heddon Valley. Reached via steep, one-in-four roads that sweep down to it on either side, this charming pub has a beautiful garden at the back that looks out over the river-threaded Heddon's Mouth Cleave to the Atlantic. It's a lovely spot to watch squirrels hop between trees and ducks waddle across the lawn while you sip a pint of one of its own-brewed Heddon Valley ales, or tuck into one of the excellent local Ruby Red steaks.

The Hunter's Inn, Heddon Valley, Parracombe, EX31 4PY. 01598 763230. thehuntersinnexmoor.co.uk

GETTING THERE

- Head west out of Lynton on the road that takes you through the Valley of Rocks. Drive past Lee Bay and keep going along the clifftop road. Around 300 metres after the Woody Bay Hotel, you'll see a parking area on the left where you can leave your vehicle.

1 Exit the car park and walk downhill, past the Woody Bay Hotel, into the wooded valley.

2 Just before the road starts going uphill again, you will see a gate on your left. Go through here and follow the track into the woods.

3 Turn right onto a lane after 10 minutes or so, and follow it all the way down to the beach.

4 To continue with our suggested circular route, walk back up the lane from the beach, past the point at which you joined it.

5 When you reach the road at the top, turn right and you will see the parking area ahead of you.

SUNBATHING

SECLUSION

SWIMMING

SAND

ROCKPOOLS & CAVES

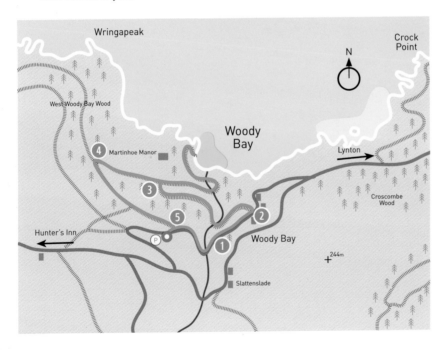

EBB & FLOW

There's an expansive area of soft sand at low tide, as well as a large pool, flat rocks and an old lime kiln to explore. You can even shower in the waterfall at the back of the beach. Much of the beach is still accessible when the sea comes in.

198

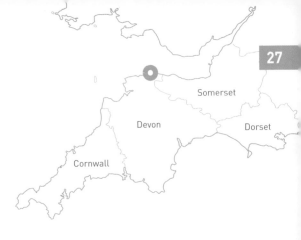

Somerset

Devon

Dorset

Cornwall

Descend into the basket-shaped hollow of Wringcliff Bay, below Devon's famous Valley of Rocks, and a sense of otherworldliness sweeps over you. This could be to do with the moonscape feel of the dark sand and lead-coloured stone beneath your feet or the granite slabs of Castle Rock and Rugged Jack Rock towering overhead. But it's just as likely caused by the way this tiny, difficult-to-reach cove muffles out the bird twitter and wind ripple of the landscape above. Our suggested walk is easy to follow, but requires some sure-footed clambering on the near-vertical climb down to the beach. Expect a serious cardio-vascular workout on the way back up, too.

| EX35 6JH | THE WALK 2.5km / 45mins | BEACH ACCESS | SS 701,496 |

THE PITSTOP

Named after a character from RD Blackmore's Exmoor-set novel *Lorna Doone*, Mother Meldrum's Tea Room is a cosy and welcoming place to stop amid the bleak landscape of the Valley of Rocks. It may be a little on the touristy side – expect to be plied with Rugged Jack scones and Castle Rock cakes – but its leafy, shaded garden is a perfect spot to cool down after a day of baking sun on the beach. If you time it right, you might even catch a game of cricket on the pitch next door.

Mother Meldrum's Tea Gardens, Valley of Rocks, Lee Road, near Lynton, EX35 6JH. 01598 753667

GETTING THERE

Head west out of Lynton and follow signs for the Valley of Rocks. As you enter the valley – it's aptly named, so you'll know when you do – park in the second car park just after the cricket pitch and restaurant.

1 Walk out of the car park, and head downhill on the shingle pathway towards the roundabout.

2 On the far side of the roundabout, you will see a path that leads downhill past Castle Rock. Follow this.

3 When the bay comes into view, look for the beach-access path on the right.

4 Once you've visited the beach, simply retrace your steps back to the car park.

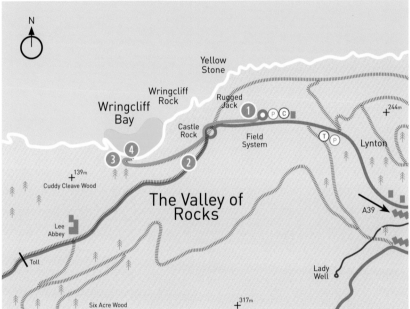

2

SUNBATHING

5

SECLUSION

2

SWIMMING

3

SAND

4

ROCKPOOLS & CAVES

EBB & FLOW

Large areas of soft sand are revealed at low tide. And there are huge, south-facing slabs of rock that are ideal for sunbathing. When the sea comes in, just a small patch of dry, grey sand remains.

South
Cornwall

Atlantic Ocean

Trevose Head

Padstow

Wadebridge

Bodmin

Towan Head

Newquay

Lostwithiel

Cornwall

St. Austell

St. Agnes

(30)

St. Austell Bay

Gribbin Head

Probus

Truro

Redruth

Dodman Point

Nare Head

Falmouth

(28)

(29)

Falmouth Bay

English Channel

Helford Estuary

Bodmin
Moor

● Tavistock

● Callington

● Liskeard

Saltash ●

● Plymouth

Crafthole ●

Whitsand
Bay

㉛ ㉜ ㉝ ㉞

Rame
Head

South Cornwall

		Page
㉘	Molunan	146
㉙	Porthbeor Beach	150
㉚	Booley Beach	154
㉛	Great Lantic Beach	158
㉜	Frog Prince Cove	162
㉝	Donkey Beach	166
㉞	Polhawn Cove	170

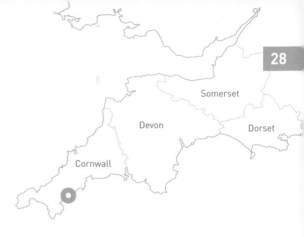
Somerset

Devon

Dorset

Cornwall

Arbitrarily divided into three sections by rocks and tides, Molunan looks out over St Anthony Head lighthouse and Pendennis Castle to the churning western extremities of the English Channel. The first, pretty section of the beach is easily reached from a car park, while the second – known as Great Molunan Beach – is a large, gently sloping section of pale mustard-coloured sand that is understandably the most popular with families looking for somewhere more tranquil than nearby Falmouth and St Mawes. The third part, Little Molunan, only shows itself at low tide, when it reveals the mouth of an incredible cave that burrows around 25 metres into the headland. When the sea is in, you can hear waves booming and drumming over its entrance, as they create sonic explosions with the trapped air. Our suggested walk takes in some wonderful Fal Estuary views, and leads you through the village of St Anthony to emerge on the wind-battered coastline at Zone Point.

TR2 5HA

THE WALK
6km
1hr 30mins

BEACH
ACCESS

SW 846,316

THE PITSTOP

St Mawes, a short ferry ride away on the other side of the estuary, has become something of an outpost of Barnes and Battersea in recent years. But, despite this gentrification, at least one good, old-fashioned pub still prospers among the delis, bistros and boutique hotels. The Victory Inn, squeezed into the steep Victory Steps, is a whitewashed, flower basket-hung tavern with outdoor wooden tables, around which fishermen and Fulhamites alike sit to drink pints of Betty Stogs and Roseland Cornish Shag while looking over the bay. This being St Mawes, it also provides an excellent seafood menu – crab risotto, homemade fish pie, beer-battered cod with handcut chips – and high-quality B&B accommodation.

The Victory Inn, Victory Steps, St Mawes, TR2 5PQ. 01326 270324. victory-inn.co.uk

If you haven't got time to take the ferry, then check out the St Anthony Head Tea Garden, situated at the start point of our suggested walk. Its scones are freshly made on the premises each day, and it serves up a selection of hot or cold lunches in its lovely, flowery garden.

St Anthony Head Tea Garden, St Anthony Head, near Portscatho, TR2 5DQ.

EBB & FLOW

All three strips of sand are exposed when the tide goes out. And, as they're within a few hundred metres of each other, it's easy to experience the very different ambience of each. When the sea comes in, only Greater Molunan is accessible. Unless the tide is particularly high, the sand remains dry and soft.

GETTING THERE

— Head south on the A3078 towards St Mawes, and turn left when you see a signpost to Gerrans and Portscatho. Follow the road all the way to its end at St Anthony Head (make sure you don't take the route to Place Barton), and park in the car park there.

1 Exit the car park and take the footpath on the right that leads to St Anthony Head lighthouse. Turn right onto the Coastal Path when you reach the bottom.

2 Walk along the path for around five minutes and, just before a footbridge, you'll see the small path that leads to the first section of beach. If you want to do a shorter walk of around one kilometre, simply go right here and climb the steps back to the car park.

3 If you want to continue to the second – larger – section, carry on along the path for a further 200 metres, and you'll see the access path on your left. The track leading to the third section is another 200 metres along the Coastal Path, where it bends around Carricknath Point.

4 To continue with our suggested route, carry on around the Point and into a field. Bear right up the hill and into the next field on the far side of the hill.

5 When you come down the other side of the hill, join the track that leads off towards the right, and bear right after a few minutes to walk around the back of Place House. Look for the steps that will lead you down to the churchyard.

6 Walk through the cemetery, and turn left onto the lane on the other side.

7 When you near the quay for the St Mawes ferry, take the right-hand footpath that leads up the hill to Bohortha.

8 Go through the village and turn right onto the main road. After 50 metres or so, turn left onto a path – then, another 50 metres further on, turn left again onto the Coastal Path.

9 Keep walking along the Coastal Path for another half an hour, and you will reach the tip of Zone Point, where you can pause to take in the view. The car park is just 100 metres on from here.

SUNBATHING

SECLUSION

SWIMMING

SAND

ROCKPOOLS & CAVES

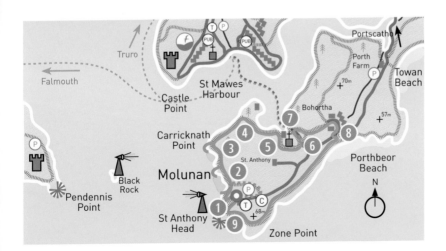

Somerset

Devon

Dorset

Cornwall

A long stretch of golden sand, Porthbeor Beach is the sort of Cornish cove that's depicted on the side of clotted-cream tubs. Despite its soft sands, wild and craggy rocks, and stunning views over the water, the beach is still a bit of a secret – and only at the highest point of high season will you have to share it with more than a handful of people. Its most fascinating feature is a crack in the northern rock outcrop, which leads into a cave fronted by its own sandy cove – accessible via a clamber over the rocks on days when the tides plug the fissure with sand. Our suggested walk takes you to the beach through farmland and over river creeks, and past the departure point for the St Mawes ferry, should you wish to hop over the water for a pint.

TR2 5EX

THE WALK
6km
1hr 30mins

BEACH
ACCESS

SW 862,320

EBB & FLOW

There's a long, wide curve of soft sand at low tide, and you can access the separate, ultra-secluded cove through a crack in the rocks at the northern end of the beach. Small sandy areas are still available when the sea comes in, and the beach emerges quickly once the water starts to retreat.

THE PITSTOP

St Mawes, a short ferry ride across the water from Porthbeor Beach, has become a seriously upmarket destination in recent years, and is popular with the sailing set who decamp here from London at weekends in search of salt air and cream teas. The elegant, white-and-blue Rising Sun pub caters firmly to this market, providing a menu of fine wines and upmarket gastropub-style cuisine – chicken with grapes in a sherry sauce, scallops in a spring onion, chive and ginger butter – that wouldn't look out of place in a Fulham freehouse. The views over St Mawes harbour and the estuary from the palm-fringed front terrace are simply wonderful; and there are eight stylish suites in which you can prolong your stay should you miss the ferry back.

The Rising Sun, St Mawes, TR2 5DJ.
01326 270233. risingsunstmawes.co.uk

GETTING THERE

— Head south on the A3078 towards St Mawes, then turn left at the signpost to Gerrans and Portscatho. Follow the road through Gerrans and, just after you pass the river creek around two kilometres further on, you will see a car park at Porth Farm. Leave your vehicle here.

1 Turn left out of the car park and walk for around 50 metres, then turn onto the footpath on your right. Just before you reach Towan Beach, turn right again onto the Coastal Path.

2 Walk along this path for 25 minutes or so, until Porthbeor beach comes into view. Go through a gate and, around 200 metres further on, go down the steps on your left.

3 To continue with our suggested circular route, climb back up the steps and take the path that leads straight ahead to the road. Turn right, then left onto a small lane after around 50 metres.

4 If you'd like to cut the walk short at this point, you can simply follow the road back to the car park.

5 To continue, follow the lane around the bend and onto the track that leads straight ahead. Carry on along this until it turns into a pathway and heads out towards some fields. Take the right-hand fork when it splits and walk downhill.

6 When you reach the creek, turn right and walk past the ferry quay. Follow the track as it winds around the banks of the estuary and into Porth Creek.

7 Once you have passed over a footbridge, turn right and follow the path for 200 metres or so back to the car park at Porth Farm.

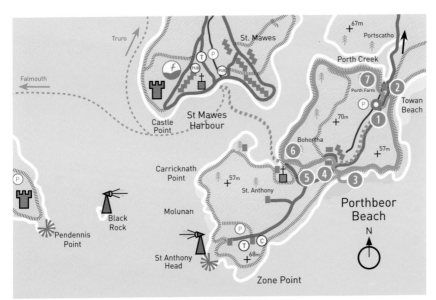

4
SUNBATHING

4
SECLUSION

4
SWIMMING

5
SAND

5
ROCKPOOLS & CAVES

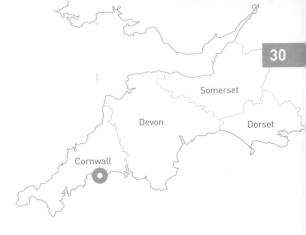
Nestling into green-fronted cliffs between the popular beaches of Par Sands and Polkerris, Booley Beach makes a peaceful alternative to either. Though one of Cornwall's most popular walking routes passes behind it, few venture down onto the sizeable strip of pale-yellow sand and pebbles. More fool them. This quiet beach is ideal for lazy, sun-drenched afternoons and evening barbecues in front of a sun-pinkened horizon. Our suggested walk is an undemanding stroll over a small headland, which takes in some gorgeous views as well as an equally lovely pub.

PL24 2TL

THE WALK
2km / 25mins

BEACH ACCESS

SX 088,524

THE PITSTOP

With a large sun terrace situated directly above the beach at Polkerris, The Rashleigh Inn is understandably popular. Its location means that a lazy landlord could turn a tidy profit even if they sold just fizzy lager and pork scratchings, so it's to Jon and Samantha Spode's credit that the Rashleigh is up there with Cornwall's finest pubs. There are usually around six local ales – including Otter Bitter, Betty Stogs and St Austell HSD – on draught at any one time, and inventive menus feature the likes of slow-baked steak-and-ale pie and Fowey river mussels in a leek-and-cider sauce. Children are well-served, too. Kids' meals of plaice goujons and chips are wittily presented in sandcastle buckets.

The Rashleigh Inn, Polkerris, PL24 2TL. 01726 813991. rashleighinnpolkerris.co.uk

GETTING THERE

— Drive east out of Par on the A3082 towards Fowey, then take the right-hand turn to Polkerris just after the bend in the road. Follow the road downhill and, after 200 metres or so, turn left into the car park, which costs £2.50.

1 Exit the car park, turn right and walk towards the harbour. Just before you reach The Rashleigh Inn, turn right and join the Coastal Path where it runs along the front of a row of terraced cottages. As you climb up the headland, look behind you for a fantastic view of Polkerris harbour.

2 Booley Beach will come into view around 200 metres after you've reached the top of the headland. Walk along the Coastal Path to the far side, and turn down the pathway that leads to the beach.

3 To return to the car park, simply retrace your steps.

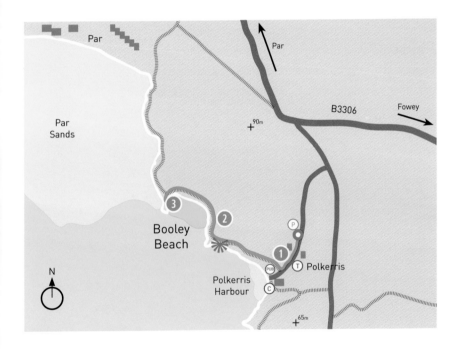

SUNBATHING

SECLUSION

SWIMMING

SAND

ROCKPOOLS & CAVES

EBB & FLOW

When the tide is out, there's a large beach area with patches of sand in between the pebbles. The sand at the front can be wet, so sunbathers should look for a spot nearer the cliffs. At high tide, just a small and predominantly pebbled area of beach remains.

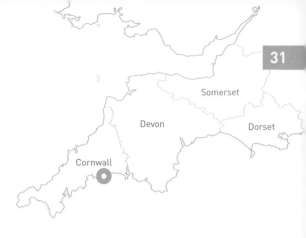

Somerset

Devon

Dorset

Cornwall

A miniature – and far less busy – version of Kynance Cove, Great Lantic Beach offers the same sweeping expanse of pale sand as its popular counterpart down on the Lizard peninsula. And, even better, it leads onto a fascinating network of smaller and even more secluded beaches that can be accessed either on foot or by a short swim. The tides here have exercised an eerily accurate sorting technique, and the beach has been naturally graded into sections that go from fine sand at the back to large pebbles at the front, all of which lends the terrain a muted rainbow effect. Our suggested circular walk can be completed in less than half an hour, though you should steel yourself for a steep climb back up the headland from the beach.

PL23 1NP   THE WALK   BEACH   SX 147,508
          2km / 30mins ACCESS

THE PITSTOP

A traditional, stone-built building that overlooks the harbour at Polruan, The Lugger Inn is situated just two-and-a-half kilometres further along the Coastal Path from Great Lantic Beach. Inside, it's a proper pub – in the low-ceilinged, dark-beamed and locals-frequented sense of the words – with a good selection of draught beers from the St Austell brewery. Food-wise, it doesn't stray far from the pub grub template, but it does the staples – steak-and-ale pie, chicken curry, fish and chips – very well indeed. Look out for the regular live-music sessions, too.

The Lugger Inn, The Quay, Polruan, PL23 1PA. 01726 870007. luggerinnpolruan.co.uk

GETTING THERE

— Leave Polruan on the only road out of the village and go up the hill. Take the third road on the left after around two miles and turn into Pencarrow car park, which is immediately on the right.

1 Exit the car park, then turn left and join the pathway on the other side of the road.

2 Turn left when you enter a field and walk along the boundary hedge until you meet the Coastal Path. Turn right down the hill.

3 Follow the path for 50 metres or so, then turn left through the gate.

4 Go down the set of steep steps and, just before you reach the next gate, turn right onto the beach-access path.

5 To return to your car, simply retrace your steps.

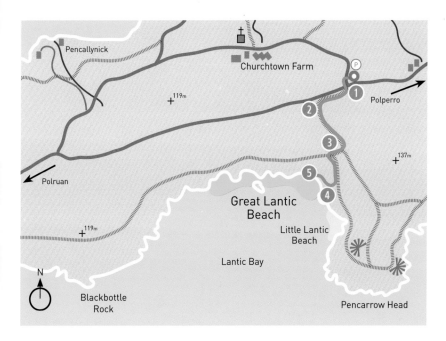

SUNBATHING

SECLUSION

SWIMMING

SAND

ROCKPOOLS & CAVES

EBB & FLOW

The secluded sections of the beach are all accessible at low tide. You may well have to swim back if you hang about for too long, though. The main beach retains a large area of soft, dry sand in all but the highest of tides and most extreme storms.

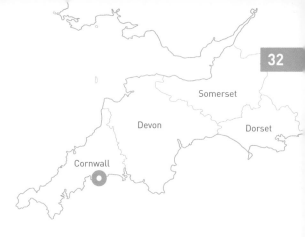
Somerset

Devon

Dorset

Cornwall

Overlooked by Ordnance Survey, and unmarked on any map or chart, this tiny strip of sand is so secret that we've had to make up our own name for it. Frog Prince Cove, though, is very apt; encompassing not just the beach's fairytale ambience, but also its proximity to the hamlet of Frogmore and the amphibian-shaped rock that stands nearby. The jewel-like blue water off this sandy inlet is ideal for wild swimming, and adjacent Palace Cove is just a 100-metre freestyle splash away, past plenty of smooth-sand resting places and jump-perfect rocks. Our suggested short walk is one of the least taxing in this book, and the easy beach access makes it ideal for families.

PL23 1NP   THE WALK   BEACH   SX 159,511
             2km / 25mins   ACCESS

THE PITSTOP

Something of a time capsule, The Old Ferry Inn at Bodinnick-by-Fowey – just a short drive away from Frogmore – looks, in 2015, almost exactly as it would have done in 1815. The intimate, oak-panelled bar, with its brass draught pumps and ships' lanterns suspended from the ceiling provides the atmosphere, while the River Fowey outside supplies the wow factor. Beer is from Sharp's Brewery, just along the coast in Rock, and many a thirsty walker has stopped here to watch boats negotiate the mouth of the estuary while nursing a pint of Cornish Coaster. The food – plaice goujons, home-battered haddock, lamb shank with mint-and-onion gravy – is of the upmarket pub grub variety, and there's also great ice-cream to take away.

The Old Ferry Inn, Bodinnick-by-Fowey, PL23 1LX. 01726 870237. oldferryinn.co.uk

GETTING THERE

— Drive away from Polruan on the only road out of the village, then go up the hill and past two left turns. A couple of kilometres after the second of these, you will arrive at a sharp bend in the road. The car park at Frogmore is on the left just after this.

1 Follow the path that begins across the road from the car park entrance. Continue over the lane and, after a couple of minutes, you will reach a field.

2 Take the path that crosses the field diagonally towards the far right-hand corner. Halfway along this path, you'll see a path that leads off to the left. Follow this past a bench and, after a few minutes, take the beach access pathway on your left.

3 To return to the car park, simply retrace your steps.

SUNBATHING

SECLUSION

SWIMMING

SAND

ROCKPOOLS & CAVES

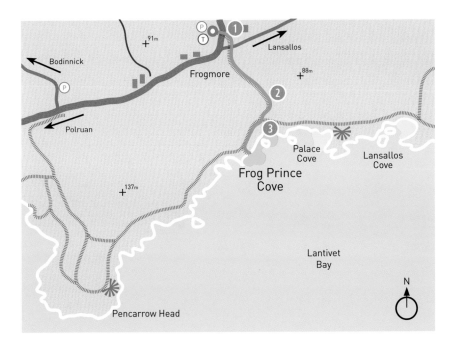

EBB & FLOW

There are many miniature beaches scattered around this small area, and the rocks that separate them are easy to clamber over or wade around when the tide is out. When water levels rise, only the small area of sand next to the beach-access path remains accessible. If you swim to the left, though, you can find more dry sand in a larger inlet.

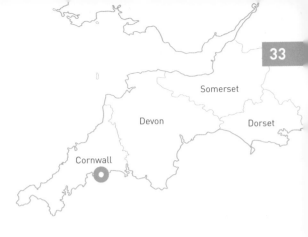

Somerset

Devon

Dorset

Cornwall

The name of this tiny slip of beach, part of the wider Talland Bay, is a little misleading. Though it's ideal for children – and, indeed, our short, suggested walk doesn't demand too much of little feet – there are no rainbow-haltered, equine trudgers here; just talcum-soft sand, colourful rockpools and some wonderful wild swimming opportunities amid the cobalt-coloured lagoons. Though it's a world away from the busy shore at nearby Polperro, Donkey Beach is so small that it can feel crowded when just a few people take to the sand. Get there early to claim a spot before in-the-know locals do.

| PL13 2JA | THE WALK 3.5km / 50mins | BEACH ACCESS | SX 222,510 |

THE PITSTOP

Though its name suggests a creaky-timbered pub, the Smugglers Rest is actually a rather genteel licensed café with the sort of sun terrace on which people sip Pimms rather than pints. That's not to say they don't do beer. There are refreshing lagers on tap all year round, and in high season the proprietors bring in barrels of Cornish ale, too. Open during the day for breakfasts (including one fry-up ominously known as The Gladiator) and light meals of the crab sandwich ilk, it hosts occasional barbecues on summer evenings at which everything from burgers and steaks to shark and swordfish gets the flame-grilled treatment.

Smugglers Rest, Talland Bay, near Looe, PL13 2JA. 01503 272259

GETTING THERE

— Drive west on the A387 from Looe and follow signs to Portlooe. At the T-junction after 300 metres, turn right to Talland. Leave your vehicle either in the free car park at the bottom of the hill or outside the Smugglers Rest café. If both are full, there is another car park at the Talland Beach Café (£2.50).

1 Walk along the lane towards Talland Beach from the free car park or the Smugglers Rest, then turn left when you see signs to Talland Beach Café.

2 Go past the toilets and the café, and take the left-hand turning just as the lane starts to climb uphill.

3 Halfway up the hill, turn onto the path that leads off to the left. When you reach a tiny lane, go left again.

4 Turn left once more when you reach the end of the lane around 250 metres further on.

5 Walk along this path for five minutes or so, then take the small offshoot pathway that leads down to the beach.

6 To continue with our suggested route, return to the path and carry on walking up it. Turn right onto a track just after you pass the war memorial.

7 Follow this track to its end, then turn right onto a lane. This will lead you back into Talland in less than 10 minutes.

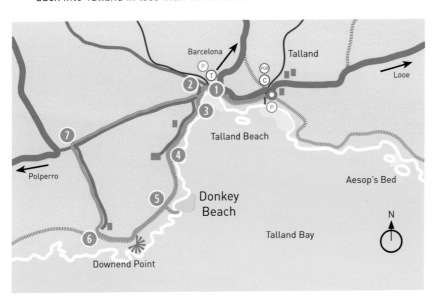

SUNBATHING

SECLUSION

SWIMMING

SAND

ROCKPOOLS & CAVES

EBB & FLOW

Only 20 metres across, this small, beautiful beach is perfect for swimming and exploring at low tide. When the tide comes in, the sand area is much smaller. Though it's still accessible if the sea is calm.

Somerset

Devon

Dorset

Cornwall

Tucked into the far, secluded end of Whitsand Bay near Rame Head, the west-facing Polhawn Cove is a wonderful place from which to watch the sunset – especially if it coincides with low tide. Here, the pastel-coloured sands spread out in a web-like pattern, and spider their way around fingers of rock that poke into the sea. It's always possible to find a secret nook in which you can enjoy absolute privacy for the day and, despite the beach's impressive width, it makes you feel as though you've stumbled across a hidden inlet. Our long suggested walk takes you down to the beach in around 15 minutes before leading you up sleepy lanes, into a village pub and along the tumbledown clifftops.

PL10 1LH

THE WALK
8km / 2hrs

BEACH
ACCESS

SX 420,495

EBB & FLOW

There's plenty of fine, soft sand in the areas between rocky outcrops at low tide; and the beach is still easily accessible when the sea comes in. Expect to find lots of dry sand during all but the highest of tides.

THE PITSTOP

On warm summer evenings, The Cross Keys Inn in Cawsand feels positively Provençal. People spill out of the lively bar into the village square, clutching glasses of wine, and all the scene seems to lack is the clink and click of petanque balls. Popular with sailing enthusiasts due to its position at the entrance to Plymouth harbour, this upmarket pub mixes salty maritime memorabilia with the sort of earth-toned décor you'd expect to see in a London bistro. It's certainly not snobbish though. The list of draught real ales – Summer Lightning, Keel Over, Hop Back – is enough to get any beardy CAMRA-man purring with delight, and the quality pub grub, including homemade Cornish beef burgers, is refreshingly unpretentious.

The Cross Keys Inn, The Square, Cawsand, PL10 1PF. 01752 822706.
crosskeysinncawsand.com

GETTING THERE

— Head west from Torpoint on the A374 and, at Antony, turn left onto the B3247. Go down to the T-junction and turn left, then right just after the fort. Follow the road along the clifftops to Rame. Pass through the village and follow signs to Rame Head, where you can leave your vehicle in the car park.

1 Exit the car park and go through the gate into the field after the coastguard station. Walk right along the Coastal Path and follow it past Rame Head and Queener Point.

2 Carry on along the Coastal Path past some cottages, down some steps and into a field beyond Monk Rock Cottages. Turn left down the beach-access pathway.

3 You can either retrace your steps to the car park at this point or – to continue with our suggested route – go back to Polhawn Cottage, and turn left up its driveway. Walk up to the junction and follow the lane directly ahead of you.

4 On the first bend, after 100 metres or so, turn left onto the path that leads into the field.

5 Continue until you meet another lane, then go right and immediately left onto the road.

6 At the junction, after around 250 metres, fork right and walk down to the village square in Cawsand, where you'll find the lively Cross Keys Inn.

7 After a restorative pint or two, take the lane that leads off from the right where you entered the village square. When it turns into the Coastal Path, follow it along a quiet lane and onto a path that leads around Penlee Point.

8 Continue along the path and, when near the mast next to the lifeboat station, turn off to return to your vehicle (don't follow the first sign to the car park).

SUNBATHING

SECLUSION

SWIMMING

SAND

ROCKPOOLS & CAVES

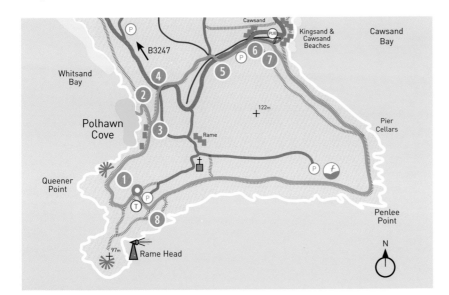

South Devon

Dartmoor
National Park

Widecombe
in the Moor

Tavistock

Princetown

Cadover Bridge

Buckfastleig

Devon

Saltash

Plymouth

Ivybridge

Newton Ferrers

35

36

37

38

Kingsbridge

Salcombe

East Prav

39

40

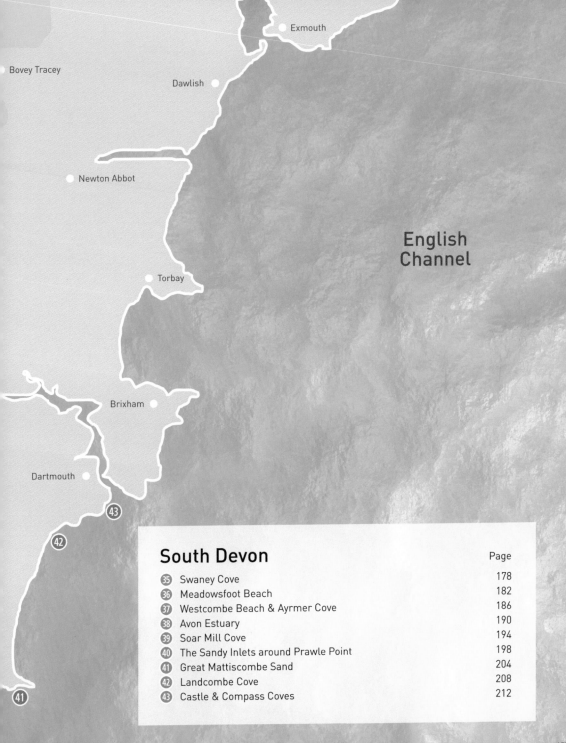

Exmouth

Bovey Tracey

Dawlish

Newton Abbot

English
Channel

Torbay

Brixham

Dartmouth

43

42

South Devon

		Page
35	Swaney Cove	178
36	Meadowsfoot Beach	182
37	Westcombe Beach & Ayrmer Cove	186
38	Avon Estuary	190
39	Soar Mill Cove	194
40	The Sandy Inlets around Prawle Point	198
41	Great Mattiscombe Sand	204
42	Landcombe Cove	208
43	Castle & Compass Coves	212

41

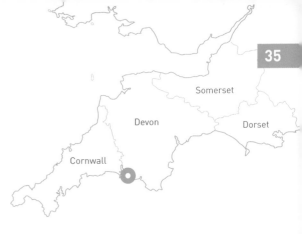

Somerset

Devon

Dorset

Cornwall

Swaney Cove is so well-kept a secret that few references to it exist on maps or the internet. This is good news for you, as it means, once you've scrambled down the rock scree to access its perfect, protected oval of pebbles at low tide, you're likely to be the only person there. We've provided several routes for our suggested walk, allowing you to take in the larger and sandier Cellar Beach nearby, and some stunning views over the mouth of the River Yealm estuary. Oh, and the fabulous Ship Inn in Noss Mayo, too.

PL8 1EL

THE WALK
9.5km
2hr 30mins

BEACH
ACCESS

SX 523,469

EBB & FLOW

When the tide is out, it leaves a small oval-shaped area of little pebbles for you to enjoy. At high tide, the beach size shrinks dramatically. Check the tidal times before you set out.

THE PITSTOP

An idyllic, white-fronted waterside building with an outdoor terrace that's almost within touching distance of boats on the River Yealm, The Ship Inn is by far the best pub in Noss Mayo. The views, obviously, are fantastic – though the bar area, sensitively renovated using reclaimed woods and other traditional materials, runs it close in the attractiveness stakes. It serves a good selection of West Country ales and ciders, and the food options – which include such gastropub staples as pan-fried duck breast on rösti potatoes and Thai green curry alongside more spit-and-sawdust pub fare like burgers and scampi – are very well executed.

The Ship Inn, Noss Mayo, PL8 1EW.
01752 872387. nossmayo.com

GETTING THERE

- Take the A379 east from Plymouth and, at Yealmpton, turn off when you see signs to Noss Mayo. Follow this road and, at Bridgend, go up the hill, bear left by the church and take the next three right-hand turns. The car park at Warren Point is around half a kilometre further on, on the left.

1 Exit the car park and follow the track that leads directly to the Coastal Path. Turn right when you climb over the stile.

2 Walk past Warren Cottage and, around 1.5 kilometres further on, you'll see a lookout post down at the front of the headland. Swaney Cove is to the left of this, though you'll need to scramble down the short slope to access it.

3 To continue with our suggested route, carry on along the Coastal Path for another 20 minutes or so until you reach a row of cottages. Take the left-hand path by the last cottage, which will lead you all the way down to Cellar Beach. The path splits at the bottom, and leads you to different sections of the shore.

4 Return to the Coastal Path and walk for 500 metres or so until you see a path to the right signposted Stoke. This is a shortcut back to the car park.

5 Alternatively, carry on along the Coastal Path and you will find yourself at The Ship Inn in Noss Mayo in less than 20 minutes.

6 After popping in for a pint, continue along the road until it starts going uphill, then bear right.

7 This road takes you past a car park and some tennis courts, and then turns into a track. When the track ends, turn left and then right to get back to your car.

SUNBATHING 3

SECLUSION 4

SWIMMING 4

SAND 2

ROCKPOOLS & CAVES 3

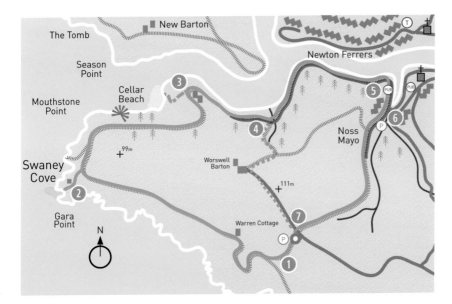

Somerset

Devon

Dorset

Cornwall

Owned and maintained by the local Flete
Estate, Meadowsfoot Beach – known locally as
Mothecombe – feels more private than most.
No doubt because public access is restricted
to Wednesdays, weekends and bank holidays.
The smooth, sandy beach, skirted by pale-green
meadows and overhung with dense woodland,
was used as a backdrop in Ang Lee's *Sense &
Sensibility* and 1970s equine fable *International
Velvet*, and its setting between idyllic English
countryside and the clear waters of the Channel
ticks all boxes that even the most pernickety
location manager could think up. A stone
fairytale cottage, built into the cliffside at one
end of the beach, only adds to the romantic
ambience. Our short, family-friendly suggested
walk offers wonderful views of the Erme
estuary, especially at low tide.

PL8 1LB

THE WALK
2km / 30mins

BEACH
ACCESS

SX 611,473

THE PITSTOP

Other than a teashop that's only open in the summer months, there's not really anywhere to stop for food and drink near Meadowsfoot Beach. So, once you've finished your walk, head inland to Holbeton, and check out upmarket pub/restaurant the Dartmoor Union. Situated at the heart of a lovely country village, this Devon Pub of the Year winner and affiliated CAMRA venue offers at least three real ales alongside an Italian-influenced menu that includes pizzas baked in a handmade wood-fired oven, classic pasta dishes and Sunday roasts. The pub is financed and run by local residents, thus ensuring quality service and ingredients.

Dartmoor Union, Fore Street, Holbeton, PL8 1NE. 01752 830346. dartmoorunion.co.uk

GETTING THERE

— Head east on the A379 from Plymouth and, after Yealmpton, follow signs to Holbeton, then Mothecombe. The beach is clearly signposted. The Flete Estate operates a large, grass car park – with its own teashop and toilets – which costs £2 between April and October.

1 Exit the car park and turn left down the road. After around 100 metres, you will see a path that leads off to the right. Follow this all the way down to the beach.

2 To continue with our suggested route, join the Coastal Path at the point where you accessed the beach and follow it around the headland. At low tide, it is possible to walk parallel to the path at beach level.

3 When you reach the road, simply follow it back up the hill to the car park. If you're coming from the beach itself, you can get to the road via a slipway.

SUNBATHING

SECLUSION

SWIMMING

SAND

ROCKPOOLS & CAVES

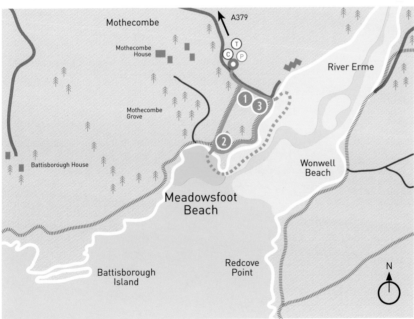

EBB & FLOW

At low tide, a large expanse of soft, golden sand stretches out, leaving rockpools at either end of the beach. Plenty of sand remains when the sea sweeps in, and the shallow waters are ideal for swimming and paddling.

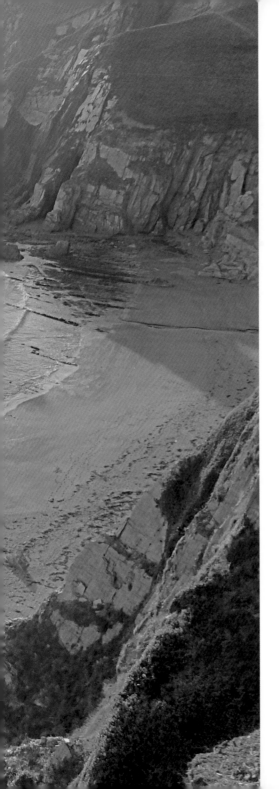

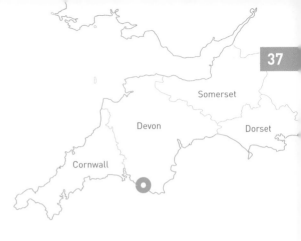

Somerset

Devon

Dorset

Cornwall

Situated just outside the popular resort of Bigbury on Sea, these two beautiful beaches make a great alternative to the people-packed sands of their bustling neighbour. Westcombe Beach, thanks to its remoter location, is the more secluded of the two – and its silvery, stream-riven sands, compressed between green, undulating cliffs, provide an excellent vantage point over where the sedate Channel starts to meet wilder western waters. Ayrmer Cove, just a short walk along the coast, may not be as sandy, but its stonier terrain leads to some wonderful rockpooling opportunities. And there are few places more atmospherically beautiful at sunset. Our suggested walk includes some steep sections of the Coastal Path, but some stunning views and a lovely 12th-century pub en route more than make up for any aching legs.

TQ7 4HR

THE WALK
5km / 2hrs

BEACH
ACCESS

Westcombe
SX 635,457
Ayrmer
SX 640,455

THE PITSTOP

With parts of its building dating back as far as 1180, the Journey's End Inn certainly has heritage. And, though it's where playwright RC Sherriff wrote the bleak, anti-war drama that gave the pub its name in the 1920s, it is as lovely and life-affirming a spot as it would have been back in flagon-swilling medieval times. A stark, white construction, outside which flower-filled hanging baskets swing gently in the sea breezes, it was serving drinks to weary travellers long before anyone dreamed up hiking boots and Goretex. Local beers are a speciality – you can expect to find the likes of Dartmoor Legend, Teignworthy Spring Tide and Otter Amber alongside the ubiquitous Doom Bar – and the selection of food is equally fine.

The Journey's End Inn, Ringmore, TQ7 4HL. 01548 810205. thejourneysendinn.co.uk

GETTING THERE

— Take the eastbound A379 in the direction of Kingsbridge, and just after Modbury, take the B3392 towards Bigbury. At St Ann's Chapel, follow the right- then left-hand signs to Ringmore. Once you're in the village, follow signs to the Ayrmer Cove car park. This costs £2.

1 Follow the path out of the end of the car park. Take the first left, which will lead you directly to Ayrmer Cove.

2 To walk on to Westcombe Beach, follow the Coastal Path westwards for around a kilometre. You will see the access point on your left.

3 To return, simply retrace your steps back to Ayrmer Cove, then take the path on your left that leads inland on the opposite side of the valley from the one you originally came down.

4 Follow this into Ringmore village. The path becomes a lane at this point.

5 Make sure you stop off for a well-deserved pint at the ancient Journey's End Inn, which is reached via a lane on the right.

6 To get back to your vehicle, carry on along the lane and follow signs to the car park.

SUNBATHING

SECLUSION

SWIMMING

SAND

ROCKPOOLS &
CAVES

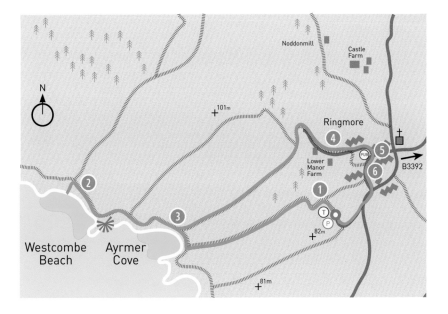

EBB & FLOW

At low tide, plenty of sand and grey shingle is revealed, as well as rockpools filled with annenomes and starfish. Lots of caves emerge, too. Both beaches shrink significantly in area at high tide, leaving mainly shingle and the occasional patch of sand.

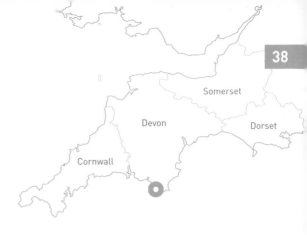

Somerset

Devon

Dorset

Cornwall

The wide mouth of the River Avon gapes at Burgh Island and the English Channel just east of Bigbury on Sea and, over the past few millennia, has carved out a landscape of sandy beaches and chiselled, grass-spattered hillsides that wind toward the sea. Thatched boathouses, from which slipways slide into the water, look out over stream-riven expanses of light-brown, while waders peck at the shallows and gulls wheel overhead. Our suggested walk along the headland gets quite steep in places, but magnificent views of the river snaking its way back towards the heart of England make it all worthwhile. Follow the directions carefully – it's easy to stray into the wrong field if you're not paying attention.

TQ7 4AR

THE WALK
3km / 30mins

BEACH
ACCESS

SX 663,442

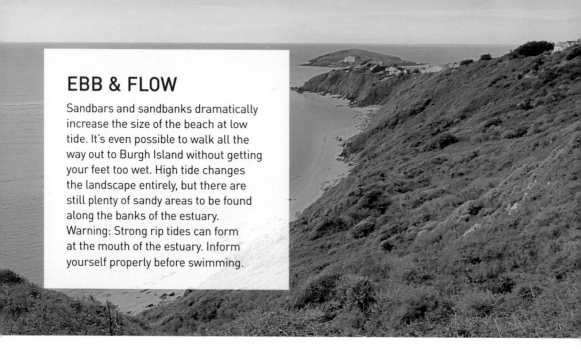

EBB & FLOW

Sandbars and sandbanks dramatically increase the size of the beach at low tide. It's even possible to walk all the way out to Burgh Island without getting your feet too wet. High tide changes the landscape entirely, but there are still plenty of sandy areas to be found along the banks of the estuary. Warning: Strong rip tides can form at the mouth of the estuary. Inform yourself properly before swimming.

THE PITSTOP

The ferry that takes passengers across the Avon Estuary to Bantham may appear infrequently – at the time of writing, it operated only between 10.00am–11.00am and 3.00pm–4.00pm six days a week, from April to September – but the long wait to return is made all the more pleasurable by The Sloop Inn. A former smugglers' haunt that dates back, in parts, to the 14th century, it is now a reassuringly old-fashioned pub in which the nautical heritage is played up to the max – there's even a rowing boat attached to the wall in the oak-panelled, stone-flagstoned bar. All the usual West Country beers and ciders are represented, and there's a decent wine list to complement the sort of dishes – fried whitebait with a herb mayonnaise, mussels in white wine and thyme, homemade fish pie – that make the wait for the boat back across the water very pleasurable indeed.

The Sloop Inn, Bantham, TQ7 3AJ.
01548 560489. thesloop.co.uk

GETTING THERE

— Take the eastbound A379 in the direction of Kingsbridge, and just after Modbury, take the B3392 towards Bigbury. Carry on through the town towards Bigbury on Sea, and park in the Mount Folly Farm car park, which is situated on the right just after the town sign.

1 Come out of the car park entrance, and follow the track that leads between the farm buildings on the other side of the road. Do not enter any fields unless you see the Coastal Path sign.

2 Follow the clifftop fence all the way down to a stile. Climb over this and continue on to a slipway.

3 At low tide, you can access the beach at this point. When the sea is in, head to the left and you'll soon come across a sandy area.

4 To return to the starting point, turn left at the slipway and walk along until you see a ferry information sign. Take the path signposted Bigbury just behind this, which leads up the headland.

5 When you reach a field, keep walking along its edge. Turn left at the top then, once you've gone through a gate, turn right onto the lane. The views from this point are simply stunning.

6 Follow the lane through part of the golf course and take the path that leads off the second bend.

7 Turn left when you meet the main road. The car park is 50 metres further on.

SUNBATHING

SECLUSION

SWIMMING

SAND

ROCKPOOLS & CAVES

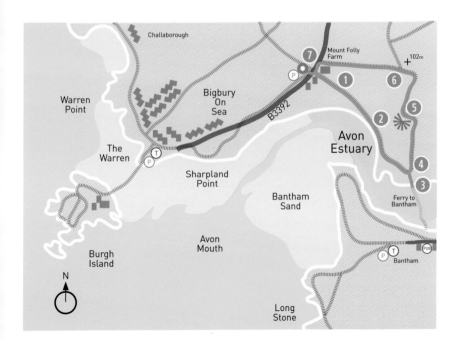

Somerset

Devon

Dorset

Cornwall

Sunset is the perfect time to visit this secluded cove, which sits beneath the looming crags of Bolt Head. Tombstone-like rocks dot the wide tranche of golden sand, casting shadows across its flat expanse as day ebbs away, while the last rosy fingers of sunlight shimmer in the surfaces of rockpools. The beach is accessed from the Coastal Path, and a hotel and campsite up on the green slopes overlooking the sands ensure a steady trickle of visitors, especially in summer. This, however, takes nothing away from its remote, ends-of-the-earth ambience. Our suggested walk takes in one of Devon's most spectacular sections of coastline – which can feel fairly demanding in places – but those with children needn't worry. The beach itself is only a short stroll from the car park.

TQ7 3DS

THE WALK
4.5km
1hr 30mins

BEACH
ACCESS

SX 697,375

EBB & FLOW

At low tide, the sea exposes huge areas
of soft sand and caves. It also reveals
two large rocks – known locally as
the Priest and the Clerk – which invite
clambering. Even when the tide is in,
there is still plenty of sand. It can bring
in a fair amount of seaweed, though,
depending on recent storms.

THE PITSTOP

If the seaweed and waves down at the cove
prove too daunting for swimming, you can
always head up the hill and take advantage of
the heated pool at the Soar Mill Cove Hotel.
Hardier types may also want to pop in to this
stylish seaside hotel for a drink or something
to eat after a dip in the briny. A glass of bubbly
while overlooking the water in the Bollinger
Bar, perhaps? Or maybe something from the
seafood-dominated menu – which includes
Salcombe scallops and chorizo salad and
sautéed fillet of Brixham seabass in a red-
pepper coulis – in the hotel's two AA
rosette restaurant?

Soar Mill Cove Hotel, near Salcombe, TQ7 3DS.
01548 561566. soarmillcove.co.uk

GETTING THERE

— Head south on the A381 to Malborough. Once you've reached the town, take the right turn signposted Bolberry. Drive along this road, following signs to Soar and then the Soar Mill Cove Hotel. The car park is situated on the left, just before the hotel.

1 Walk out of the car park and head left down the hill. Climb over the stile at the bottom and walk straight down through the fields to the beach. This should take around 10 minutes.

2 Returning from the beach, you have two options. You can either retrace your steps back to the car park or continue on our suggested walk. If you choose the latter, head over the wooden footbridge behind the beach and follow the Coastal Path eastwards around the headland.

3 After you climb over the second of two stiles, you will find yourself in a valley. When you reach the top of the other side, bear left along the wider path that leads inland.*

4 Walk along until you come to a signpost. Head in the direction of Malborough and Lower Soar, taking the path that runs through fields next to a tall farm building. Pass through three fields.

5 At the stile that leads out of the third field, you'll see the car park down in the valley to your left. Follow the path to your right, though, which winds around to the road.

6 Once you're back on the road, turn left to get to the car park.

* There are many paths in this area. They criss-cross and you will have to use your sense of direction to find your way. Look for the tall farm building as a marker.

SUNBATHING

SECLUSION

SWIMMING

SAND

ROCKPOOLS & CAVES

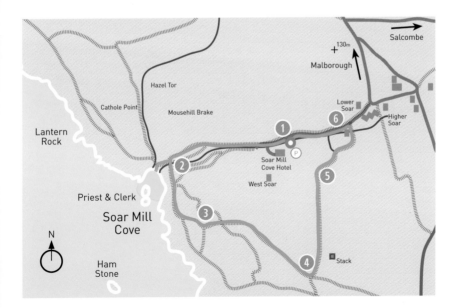

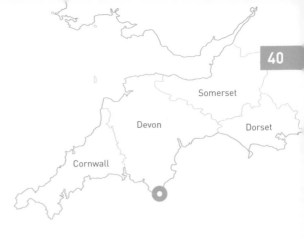

Somerset

Devon

Dorset

Cornwall

It's easy to see why the coves around Prawle Point were used as locations in the iconic Comic Strip Presents... episode *Five Go Mad In Dorset*. With their butter-coloured sand, craggy backdrop and sun-soaked, south-facing aspect, they look almost as though they've been dreamt up by Enid Blyton. Elender Cove and Macely Beach sit almost within touching distance of each other on a heart-shaped bay, while Moor Sands, just up the coastline, has as many pebbles as it does soft sand. Our suggested two-hour walk takes in some particularly breathtaking sections of the Coastal Path, but it does include a few challenging scrambles over rocks. It's well worth it, though.

| TQ7 2BY | THE WALK 7.5km / 2hrs | BEACH ACCESS M | Macely Beach SX 766,357 Elender Cove SX 769,356 | Moor Sands SX 762,363 |

THE VILLAGE & THE POINT

If one village in this book deserves a section to itself, it's East Prawle. You would have thought that a tiny settlement tucked away at the bottom of a Devon peninsula would be sleepier than a drugged koala, but this South Hams hamlet has a vibrancy to rival most cities. It even has even a Banksy rat sprayed next to the phone box. The local, The Pig's Nose Inn, hosts raucous gigs by some of Britain's most well-known bands – and no one in the village asks them to turn it down a bit – and the nearby Piglet Café continues the porcine theme, and does some great bacon and sausages with its Full English. Prawle Point, a windswept finger of land pointing out into the Channel, has to be one of the most breathtaking spots on the south coast. Heading up there is like playing a game of Russian roulette with the elements; you could just as easily be picnicking in a gale as you could be basking in glorious sunshine and enjoying the outstanding views.

THE PITSTOP

Dating back 500 years, the wonderfully named Pig's Nose Inn in East Prawle was once a favourite of the smugglers who rolled barrels of illegal booty onto the local beaches. It serves more pints than tots of rum these days, but the pub stills retains a gloriously old-fashioned feel. The slate-and-whitewash exterior gives onto a bar area in which lanterns, bottled ships, flags and fairylights hang over those drinking real ale at the bar or devouring cod and chips at the wooden tables. It's also got an enviable reputation for live music. The Animals, the Yardbirds and, erm, Curiosity Killed the Cat have all performed there in recent years.

Pig's Nose Inn, East Prawle, TQ7 2BY.
01548 511209. pigsnoseinn.co.uk

GETTING THERE

— Head east on the A379 and turn right at the mini roundabout after Chillington. This road will take you all the way to East Prawle. Parking at the village green is free, but drivers are invited to make a donation to the local church fund. Extra parking spots and other pathways are marked on the map so you can opt to take a shorter route.

1 Exit the car park and head down the lane that leads away from the village, which is signposted to Prawle Point. Walk for around five minutes and, on the sharp bend, take the path ahead of you.

2 At the crossways, turn left towards the Coastal Path. When you join the path, either turn right to get to Moor Sands, or left to visit Macely Beach and Elender Cove.

3 Moor Sands is very easy to find. Walk for 10 minutes or so along the Coastal Path and cross over a footbridge. The access pathway begins on the other side of the hillock in front of you.

4 To get to Macely Beach, walk the other way up the Coastal Path for around 100 metres, and you will see the access path on your right. The path leading to Elender Cove is five minutes further along the Coastal Path on the right.

5 To continue with our suggested route, carry on along the Coastal Path past Macely Beach and Elender Cove. Walk for 45 minutes, passing the lookout post at Prawle Point and rounding Sharper's Head.

6 At the back of Horseley Cove, turn left onto the pathway that leads inland. Continue for around five minutes, then turn right onto a path through a field (be careful, it's easy to miss). At the top of the field, turn right and follow the path, which becomes a road that takes you back to your car.

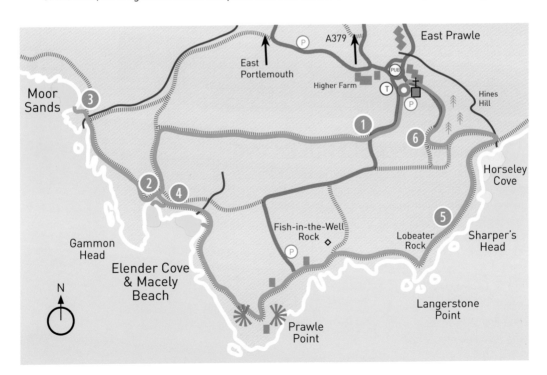

5

SUNBATHING

3

SECLUSION

5

SWIMMING

5

SAND

2

ROCKPOOLS &
CAVES

MACELY BEACH & ELENDER COVE

These two secluded, sandy slips form the curves at the top of a heart-shaped
bay, and are close enough to swim between when the sea is calm. Though
they're popular with in-the-know locals – who come here for the fine, soft
sand – the steep access paths deter most, and prevent them from ever getting
too crowded.

EBB & FLOW

As both Macely Beach and Elender Cove are tidal beaches, they cease to exist
when the sea comes in. Time your walk to take advantage to the large areas of
sand revealed at low tide.

SUNBATHING

SECLUSION

SWIMMING

SAND

ROCKPOOLS &
CAVES

MOOR SANDS

Set slightly away from the standard walking trails around Prawle Point,
Moor Sands – also known as Venerick's Cove – is a favourite of naturists,
and is certainly secluded enough for you to strip off completely. But, as it's usually
pretty deserted, you won't get frowned at if you don't fancy bearing all. The small
pebbles won't hurt your feet if you skip into the sea in your birthday suit, though.

EBB & FLOW

The beach still offers a small area of sand at high tide – though it will most
likely be wet and covered in seaweed. Take time out on the grassy headland
if you arrive at high water.

41 Great Mattiscombe Sand

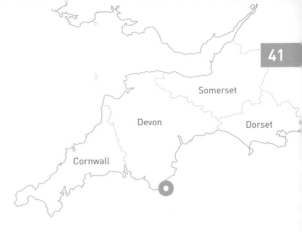
A genuinely secluded sweep of pale-brown sand and smooth pebbles, Great Mattiscombe offers some seriously impressive rock formations. Dotted along the shoreline, these tall and twisted natural henges can look – as the sun dips below the horizon – like something from a Dalí painting, and provide the beach with an eerie, otherworldly beauty. Our suggested walk, which throws up some breathtaking views across the water to Dartmouth and Slapton Sands, takes you around the rugged headland of Start Point and along some of the more rudimentary sections of the Coastal Path. Watch your footing.

TQ7 2ET

THE WALK
3km / 35mins

BEACH
ACCESS

SX 817,369

THE PITSTOP

Though it's a good 10 minutes' drive away, the Tradesman's Arms in Stokenham is a great stopping-off point on your way back from the beach. A flower basket-festooned, thatched inn that dates, in part, back to the 14th century, it serves a good selection of beers and real ales – including several from the surrounding area. It has a good reputation for food, too; and its kitchens make excellent use of fresh locally sourced meat and fish. Make sure you try the hand-dived scallops on crispy belly pork or the classic fish pie, made from fresh seafood landed in the nearby coastal villages.

The Tradesman's Arms, Stokenham, TQ7 2SZ.
01548 580996. thetradesmansarms.com

GETTING THERE

— Take the A379 to Stokenham and then follow signs to Start Point. These will guide you all the way to the car park. Parking costs £3.

1 Follow signs to Start Point from the car park. About halfway along the path to the lighthouse, you will see a path leading off to the right. This takes you along the southern edge of Start Point and then to the beach.

2 For a scenic diversion from our suggested route, simply walk down to the lighthouse and back – it only takes an extra 10 minutes.

3 The beach can be found around 15 minutes or so along the Coastal Path. The access track that leads directly down to the sands is easily spotted.

4 To get back to your car, return to the Coastal Path and look for the sign just behind the beach that directs you to the car park. Walk for around a kilometre back to your vehicle.

4

SUNBATHING

4

SECLUSION

4

SWIMMING

3

SAND

4

ROCKPOOLS & CAVES

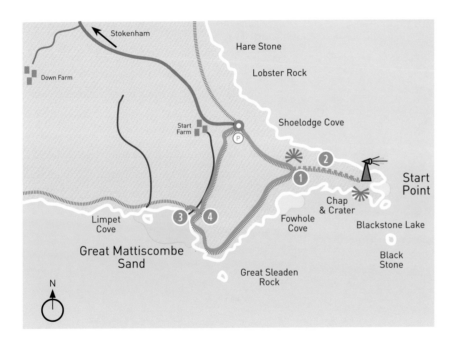

EBB & FLOW

At low tide, the pebbly areas are comfortable to sit on and there's plenty of shade in which to relax. Though the beach shrinks radically at high tide, it's still worth a visit. The grassy headland that overlooks it makes a lovely stopping place when the water's high.

Somerset

Devon

Dorset

Cornwall

Beaches don't get much more secret than Landcombe Cove – situated between crowded Slapton and Blackpool Sands. A steep descent to the shore deters all but the most dedicated beach-lovers and, unless you're visiting on a summer weekend, you're likely to have the entire place to yourself. Secluded enough even for naturists, the large crescent of smooth pebbles offers plenty of stretching-out space – even at high tide – and incorporates several caves and a secretive, annexe-like patch that can only be accessed when the sea is out. Our suggested walk, which begins in the village of Strete, might be easygoing to begin with, but it requires stout calves as you make your way down to the toffee-coloured shore. Getting back up afterwards takes some effort, too.

| TQ6 0RN | THE WALK 3km / 35mins | BEACH ACCESS | SX 850,472 |

THE PITSTOP

With its fancy filigreed façade, the King's Arms in Strete looks as though it would be better suited to New Orleans than a small Devon village. But it makes up for this discrepancy by laying on a proudly southwestern selection of beers and ciders, and a menu that makes excellent use of local seafood. Feted by *The Times* and *The Daily Telegraph* for its Brixham mussels, Bigbury Bay oysters and upmarket dishes such as pan-fried fillet of halibut on a roasted pepper and aubergine ragout, this is in a different league to most seaside boozers. Its extensive wine list means you can opt for Rioja or Riesling over real ale if you wish.

The King's Arms, Dartmouth Road, Strete, TQ6 0RW. 01803 770377.
kingsarms-dartmouth.co.uk

GETTING THERE

— Head south on the A379 from Dartmouth and, just before you reach Strete, you will see parking bays on the left-hand side of the road. If these are full, you can leave your vehicle in the car park at the King's Arms pub. Make sure you pop in to buy a drink on your way back though.

1 The Coastal Path runs into a field beside the parking bays. Head in the opposite direction from Strete and follow it for 10 minutes or so.

2 You will pass through an area of tall heather and scrub, and, after 15 minutes, enter a steep valley. At this point, you'll see Landcombe Cove and the path leading down to it.

3 Follow the path down the hill to your right and, when it starts getting really steep, bear to the left and turn right onto the track that runs alongside an old wall.

4 To return to your car, simply retrace your steps back up the hill and along the Coastal Path.

SUNBATHING

SECLUSION

SWIMMING

SAND

ROCKPOOLS & CAVES

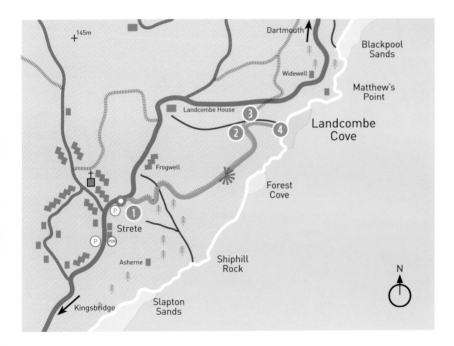

EBB & FLOW

At low tide, the beach offers plenty of space, but its surface of tiny, sea-polished pebbles drops off sharply into the water. Though the area of the beach is reduced by the incoming tide, sections around the access path remain unsubmerged.

Somerset

Devon

Dorset

Cornwall

These two adjoining beaches – one of which takes its name from the 14th-century castle that sits above them – are ideal for escaping the hubbub of nearby Dartmouth. Both are sheltered, secluded and swimmer-friendly, and though they're overlooked by towers and turrets – and, in summer, many a tourist – they remain seldom visited. Tiny Castle Cove is a mixture of pale-grey rock and shingle, while Compass, from which you can gaze out at the point where the River Dart widens into the English Channel, is comprised of dust-soft sand that leads onto seaweed-slicked boulders. Our short suggested walk takes in some particularly stunning views of the Dart estuary.

TQ6 0JN

THE WALK
2.5km / 35mins

BEACH
ACCESS

Castle Cove
SX 886,502
Compass Cove
SX 884,493

EBB & FLOW

Castle Cove is small and irregularly shaped, with extra splatterings of sand around the rocks to its right. Compass Cove is a large, perfectly curved slip of beach at low tide, offering plenty of sand. Both are mainly submerged at high tide, so time your visits carefully.

THE PITSTOP

Situated just back from the riverfront in Dartmouth, the Cherub Inn is as old-fashioned a pub as any you'll find in Devon. Housed in a 14th-century, Grade II-listed building fashioned from old ship timbers, and hung with colourful flower baskets, it looks almost exactly as it would have done when those milling about on the pavements outside chattered in Middle English. Its approach to beer is equally traditional, and real ales on draught include the likes of Otter Best and Proper Job. Upstairs, there's a restaurant that serves a seafood-heavy selection of local dishes – Dartmouth chowder, mussels poached in Orchard cider and Devon cream, homemade fish cakes – which, though slightly pricey, are very well executed.

The Cherub Inn, 13 Higher Street, Dartmouth, TQ6 9RB. 01803 832571. the-cherub.co.uk

GETTING THERE

— Head south towards Warfleet from Dartmouth on the B3205. When you reach the village, take the turning on the left to Dartmouth Castle, then bear right when the road splits. Drive as far as you can along this road, and park on the verge near the turning area.

1 Take the flight of stairs from the turning area, which leads you down to the castle. A further flight of stairs will take you down to Castle Cove.

2 For Compass Cove, come back up the steps and turn left along the road, passing the turning area. This leads onto a path that takes you to a gate and stile.

3 Climb over the stile and enter a valley, from which you'll be able to see several paths snaking down to the shore. All of these lead to a stile at the bottom of the hill. Scale this stile and turn right to access Compass Cove.

4 To continue with our suggested route, turn left at the stile and follow the Coastal Path. This leads back to the road near the turning area.

	Castle Cove	Compass Cove
SUNBATHING	3	4
SECLUSION	2	4
SWIMMING	5	4
SAND	3	3
ROCKPOOLS & CAVES	5	3

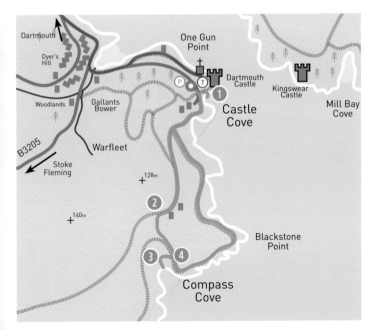

Jurassic Coast

Cullompton

Chard

Honiton

Beaminster

Devon

Axminster

Lyme Regis

Bridport

Seaton

46

Sidmouth

44   45

Exmouth

Jurassic Coast

		Page
44	Littlecombe Shoot	220
45	Hooken Beach	224
46	Cogden Beach	228
47	White Nothe Beach	232
48	Mupe Bay	236
49	Chapman's Pool	240
50	Shipstal Beach & the Arne Nature Reserve	244

Dorset

Hermitage

Blandford Forum

Bere Regis

Dorchester

Wareham

Poole

50

Corfe

Weymouth

47

48

Swanage

49

English
Channel

Somerset

Devon

Dorset

Cornwall

Tucked beneath rust-red Triassic Cliffs that swoop down the coast to Exmouth and beyond, Littlecombe Shoot on the Devon-Dorset border is such a well-guarded secret that the only company you're likely to have on its long, pebbly sweep are old fishermen's huts and gnarled pieces of driftwood. Here, the smooth, tiny stones have been sifted and sorted by the tides into an immense, Japanese garden-style pattern, which just adds to the beach's peaceful, Zen-like nature. Our glorious suggested walk leads you from the idyllic village of Branscombe through woodland down to the shoreline of the English Channel. The views, unsurprisingly, are spectacular.

EX12 3AQ | THE WALK 6.5km 1hr 30mins | BEACH ACCESS | SY 187,879

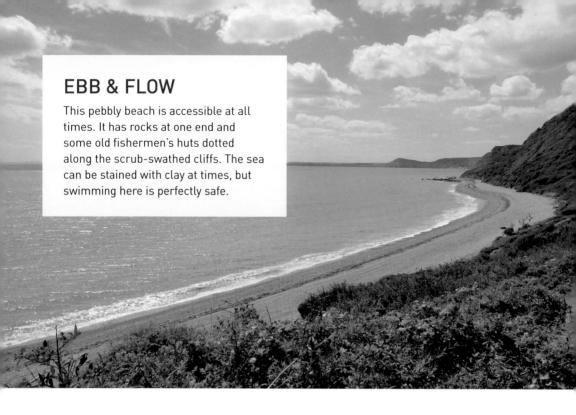

EBB & FLOW

This pebbly beach is accessible at all times. It has rocks at one end and some old fishermen's huts dotted along the scrub-swathed cliffs. The sea can be stained with clay at times, but swimming here is perfectly safe.

THE PITSTOP

With wisteria-clad walls and thatched sections of roof, The Mason's Arms in Branscombe has to be a contender for one of England's prettiest pubs – never mind East Devon's. Inside, it's a similar story. Drinkers stand beneath ancient beams on a slate floor, and lean against stone walls as they gulp from pints of St Austell ales and Thatcher's cider. Much more than just a local inn, it also offers accommodation and high-quality dining in a dedicated restaurant. Chef Scott Garland sources almost all of his ingredients locally – lobster and crab usually come from Branscombe beach – and his creations, which include salmon, mussel, haddock and leek stew, and twice-baked savoury cheesecake, are delicious.

The Mason's Arms, Branscombe Village, EX12 3DJ. 01297 680300. masonsarms.co.uk

GETTING THERE

- Head east on the A3052 from Sidmouth and take the right-hand turn at Branscombe Cross. Drive down the road and, after around 1.5 kilometres, turn left into Branscombe. Leave your vehicle in the village hall car park, and drop a donation into the well.

1 Head back up the hill, take the pathway into the cemetery and walk around the back of the church. Bear right onto the path that leads over the stream and into the woods.

2 Exit the woods and turn right onto the track. After 400 metres, turn left onto the Weston Mouth track. At a clearing, take the path that leads straight ahead.

3 Follow this through a gate, then turn left onto the Bill Perriman Path, which leads you down to the beach.

4 To continue with our suggested route, walk along the beach and take the pathway that leads up the cliffs.

5 Follow this all the way to the top, then take the path signposted Berry Barton, which leads across a field.

6 Turn left when you reach the track, left onto the lane at Berry Barton Farm and, finally, after 100 metres, right onto the path that leads around the back of the farm.

7 Go through the field and down the hill, then turn left onto another lane. After around 100 metres, turn right onto the path that squeezes between two houses.

8 Walk up to the top, go through the fields and across the small, grassy airstrip, then turn right onto the lane.

9 Follow this lane as it winds down the valley toward the sea, and bear right when it meets another lane.

10 Turn left at the Post Office to return to the car park.

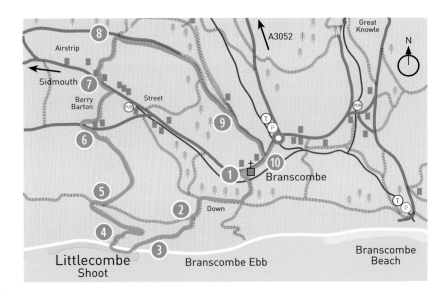

SUNBATHING 3

SECLUSION 5

SWIMMING 3

SAND 3

ROCKPOOLS & CAVES 1

Somerset

Devon

Dorset

Cornwall

Hidden under Cretaceous chalk cliffs, Hooken Beach forms a no-man's land between the Channel and the towering crags that make up the frontline of England's southern coast. Even though these bleached spires and crumbling overhangs look to be on the verge of collapse, it will be a few millennia yet before they tumble into the sea. The pebbly beach is perfect for lounging, and sun-seekers here get the double-whammy of heat beating down on the shore and reflecting off the white rock faces behind. Our suggested walk offers stunning views in both directions along the Jurassic Coast, and out to the long, fragile strip of Chesil Beach, which anchors the mainland to Portland Bill.

EX12 3AQ

THE WALK
6km
1hr 15mins

BEACH
ACCESS

SY 218,879

EBB & FLOW

This beach is an extension of Branscombe Beach – although the walk from there, over pebbles, is long and arduous. Only at the very highest of tides do you stand any chance of being cut off. Hooken Beach remains accessible and useable no matter how high the water levels.

THE PITSTOP

Strangely, for a pub that sits in the East Devon village of Beer, the Anchor Inn is as renowned for its food as its ale. It nonetheless serves up a good selection of West Country beers and ciders – including local favourite Otter Bitter – and its clifftop location, overlooking a small, pebbly section of beach and the colourful fishing boats that are moored in the shallows, guarantees a regular stream of customers wanting something to drink out in the beer garden. The dinner menu includes some inspired dishes – mushroom and spinach risotto with asparagus, seabass with a prawn and vegetable stir fry – alongside the usual Ploughmans' and gammon steaks. And it's all very affordable, too.

Anchor Inn, Fore Street, Beer, EX12 3ET.
01297 20386. oldenglishinns.co.uk

GETTING THERE

— Drive west on the A3052 and turn left onto the B3174, signposted Beer. Go through the village and down to the seafront, where the road bears to the right and climbs a steep hill. Continue for 400 metres and turn into the car park on the left. Charges vary, depending on the length of your stay.

1 Walk down the hill from the car park and take a right onto the Coastal Path after around 150 metres.

2 Follow the path along the clifftops, taking time to enjoy the views of Seaton Bay and Chesil Beach behind you. After 15 minutes or so, turn left onto the path that leads down into Under Hooken.

3 Follow this path through trees and under chalk crags until it emerges just above Hooken Beach. Walk for another few minutes and look out for the beach-access pathway on your left.

4 To continue with our suggested route, climb back up the access pathway from the beach and turn left onto the path towards Branscombe.

5 When you reach the track that goes past the beach huts, turn left. After 400 metres or so, turn right onto the path that doubles back on you and leads up the hill.

6 Walk right to the top and then head along the cliffs for around a kilometre. When you reach a tall house, take the path that leads diagonally left inland. Follow this through the fields.

7 When you reach the lane, turn right and walk down the hill back to the car park.

3
SUNBATHING

5
SECLUSION

4
SWIMMING

3
SAND

1
ROCKPOOLS & CAVES

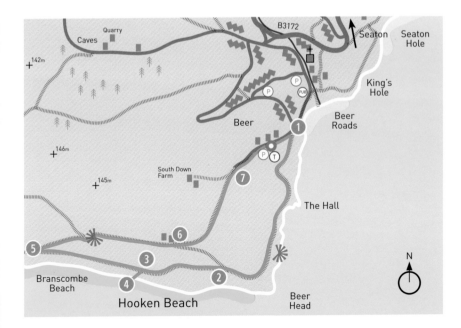

Somerset

Devon

Dorset

Cornwall

Located at the western end of the 27-kilometre, 100 million-ton pebble bank that is Chesil Beach, Cogden Beach has an unusual combination of seclusion and easy accessibility. Its lack of visitors could be due to the award-winning Hive Beach Café at next-door Burton Bradstock luring the crowds away but, whatever the reason, the handful of ramblers and anglers that do stroll its stony shore certainly don't complain. Views to the east are of the Isle of Portland and, on a clear day, you can see as far as the cliffs of Budleigh Salterton to the west. Our short suggested walk takes in some of Dorset's most dramatic coastal scenery and one of the UK's best seafood stops en route to the overhanging Burton Cliff, which is gradually dissolving into the sea.

DT6 4RL

THE WALK
4km / 1hr

BEACH
ACCESS

SY 502,881

THE PITSTOP

The Hive Beach Café, overlooking the sea just outside Burton Bradstock, is one of the UK's most fêted seafood destinations for good reason. The dishes served up in its ramshackle marquee-like dining spaces depend entirely on the catch that's been landed by local fishermen that day. Oh, and the expertise of the skilled young chefs who wield knives and pans behind its glass-fronted, fresh fish counter. It's remarkably unpretentious, too. Those pairing line-caught Portland Bill seabass with a bottle of chilled champagne are treated no differently to those who've popped in for a cup of tea and a crab sandwich. It's simply one of the best food stops in southern England.

Hive Beach Café, Beach Road, Burton Bradstock, DT6 4RF. 01308 897070. hivebeachcafe.co.uk

GETTING THERE

— Head west on the A35 out of Bridport towards Honiton, then turn onto the B3157. Drive through Burton Bradstock and past the turning for Hive Beach, then turn right into the car park after a couple of kilometres. Charges vary, depending on the length of stay.

1 Go through the gate at the bottom of the car park and walk downhill for a few minutes to Cogden Beach.

2 To continue with our suggested route, turn right and walk along the headland to Hive Beach, passing through a section of holiday park.

3 Go down the hill to the beach – making sure you stop for a drink or some fabulous fresh seafood at the Hive Beach Café – then continue along the path on the other side until you reach Burton Cliff.

4 To return, simply retrace your steps either along the headland or the beach.

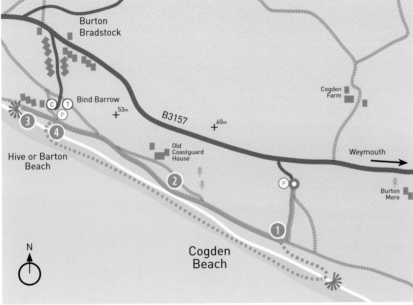

SUNBATHING

SECLUSION

SWIMMING

SAND

ROCKPOOLS & CAVES

EBB & FLOW

Tides don't change the beach too much. The flat, upper part of the beach, which supports several rare plants and flowers, is a perfect place to picnic. But be careful of the beach's steep shelf, which drops off quickly into deep water awash with very strong currents.

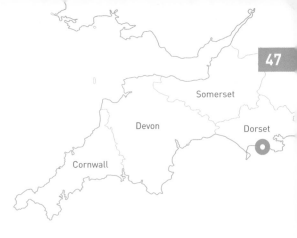

Somerset

Devon

Dorset

Cornwall

Quite how White Nothe Beach came to exist isn't really clear. A small area of boulder-surrounded pebbles, situated to the east of Weymouth, it is little more than a collection of stones that happens to have accumulated in one place. And, though we first discovered the beach back in 2009, it has such an air of transience it feels as though it could be washed away at any moment. Our challenging suggested walk takes in part of beautiful Ringstead Bay – so, if White Nothe Beach has finally given in and returned to the sea by the time you get there, you're guaranteed at least one secluded shore on which to pause. The walk also provides some wonderful views across Weymouth harbour to Portland, as well as of towering White Nothe and Burning Cliff – so called because when a portion of it crumbled away in the 19th century, the oil and tar trapped within smouldered for years afterwards.

DT2 8NQ

THE WALK
7.5km
1hr 45mins

BEACH
ACCESS

SY 766,810

EBB & FLOW

The beach is tiny at low tide and, when the sea comes in, the only accessible parts are too rocky to be of any use to you. Explore the tranquil section of shoreline beneath White Nothe until the tide starts to go out again.

THE PITSTOP

Situated just up the road from the beach at Ringstead Bay, the Ringstead Bay Kiosk may be basic, but the hot drinks and food it serves are very welcome indeed after an hour or so of scrambling across the rocks from White Nothe Beach. Famed for its fish and chips, it also chalks up a couple of reasonably priced seafood specials – fresh mackerel, crab salad – on the blackboard outside on most days. And, for those just wanting a quick bite with their mug of tea or coffee, it also dishes up cream teas and toasted teacakes.

Ringstead Bay Kiosk, Ringstead, DT2 8NG.
01305 852427

GETTING THERE

— Head southeast out of Dorchester on the A352 and turn right onto the A353. Go through Poxwell, then turn left onto the road to Upton and Ringstead just after the bend. Follow this all the way to the headland, over the cattle grid and into the National Trust car park. Make a donation.

1 Exit the car park at the far end and follow the track. When it splits, take the left-hand fork, then turn left onto the Coastal Path after around 100 metres.

2 Follow the Coastal Path up to the top of Burning Cliff and along to White Nothe Cottages. Take the right-hand fork here, then turn right along Smuggler's Path.

3 White Nothe Beach comes into view once the path starts to flatten out, and the access path is situated on the left just before a dip. You will need to scramble down for a couple of metres, but it's nothing too risky.

4 To continue with our suggested route, carry on along Smuggler's Path to the shoreline. The first part is fairly hard-going, and simply isn't possible at high tide. The second is easier, and takes you along Ringstead Bay.

5 Walk to the far side of Ringstead Bay beach and take the road that leads inland. You will pass the Ringstead Bay Kiosk after around 100 metres.

6 Continue up the road, then take the right-hand path on the first bend. Go over two stiles and a footbridge, and follow the somewhat indistinct path up the side of the valley and then on through fields past South Down Farm.

7 Keep right and follow the path up the steep gradient. You will see the car park as the path starts to flatten out.

SUNBATHING

SECLUSION

SWIMMING

SAND

ROCKPOOLS & CAVES

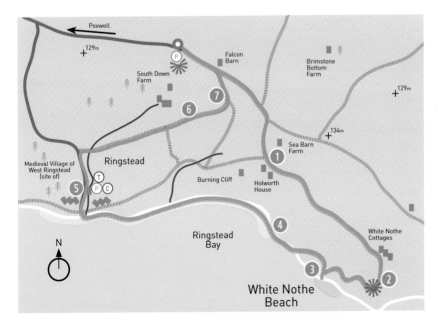

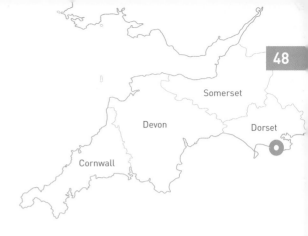

Somerset

Devon

Dorset

Cornwall

A perfect new-moon crescent of sand and small pebbles, Mupe Bay slips quietly beneath the Isle of Purbeck headlands that are used as a firing range by the Ministry of Defence. The wild swimming opportunities here are incredible and, on a still day, you can jump from teeth-like rocks that buffer the beach from the English Channel, paddle over to the left to visit several smaller beaches or explore a cave that was once used by smugglers. Our suggested walk takes you past a 'fossil forest', where long-extinct trees have been immortalised in limestone, and up to a point over Lulworth Cove for some postcard-perfect views. Reaching this vantage point requires some hard work, but the scene from the top is worth every bead of sweat.

BH20 5SE

THE WALK
7.5km
1hr 45mins

BEACH
ACCESS

SY 843,798

EBB & FLOW

Lots of soft, fine sand is revealed at low tide. Make sure you explore the Mupe Rocks, too. At high tide, the beach is still largely accessible. But there's a wooden picnic table on the flat area of headland behind the bay if the water gets too close for comfort.

THE PITSTOP

A 16th-century, white-brick building with a thatched roof and a pub sign that swings from a wooden pole, The Castle Inn at Lulworth Cove looks as though it's been built for a Hollywood film about Merrie Olde England. It's not quite as gorgeous inside, but its low beams, whitewashed walls and wood-backed public bar are atmospheric enough. And, as it's a freehouse, it serves a staggering range of West Country ales – including Fossil Fuel, Piddle and Dorset Gold – as well as the wonderfully named Cider by Rosie. Bar meals are very much of the traditional pub grub variety, though the Indian Chip Butty – garlic bread topped with chips, curry and cheese – certainly shows that someone in the kitchen isn't afraid of pushing culinary boundaries.

The Castle Inn, West Lulworth, BH20 5RN. 01929 400311. thecastleinn-lulworthcove.co.uk

GETTING THERE

— Head east on the A352 from Dorchester towards Wareham and, a kilometre or so after Owermoigne, turn right towards West Lulworth. Before you reach the main village, turn right opposite The Castle Inn onto School Lane and park wherever you find a space.

1 Take one of the pathways up the hill behind the School Lane houses. Turn left on the path at the top.

2 Once you're in a field, turn right and walk to the brow of the hill, where you will see fencing around the MOD range.

3 Go through the gate into the range and, when the path splits after around 100 metres, take the left-hand fork and follow the path along the spine of the ridge.

4 Climb over a stile and turn right down the steps. Once you've descended the hill, look for the access steps down to the beach on the far side of the bay.

5 To continue with our suggested route, go back up the access path and join the westbound Coastal Path to Lulworth Cove.

6 Climb up and over the headland at the back of Lulworth Cove, sticking to pathways closest to the cliff edge.

7 Go over a stile, then turn left onto a wider path. After around 300 metres, turn right just before a kissing gate.

8 Follow the path around the hill and, as you near houses, walk diagonally right down the hill and go through a gate.

9 Turn left onto the track and then go right onto another. Follow this track around the hill, arriving back on the path above School Lane. Find the path where you came up and descend to your car.

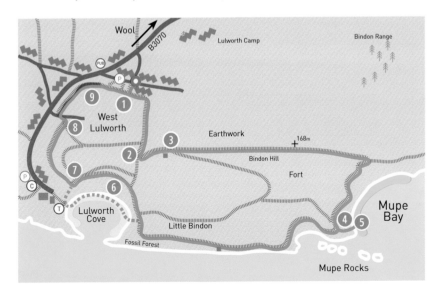

SUNBATHING

SECLUSION

SWIMMING

SAND

ROCKPOOLS & CAVES

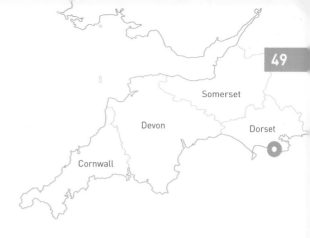

Somerset

Devon

Dorset

Cornwall

Though it rivals nearby honeypot Lulworth Cove in its shape and beauty, Chapman's Pool doesn't attract anywhere near the same numbers of visitors. The beach is well protected from currents and choppy conditions, and its gentle slope of golden sand is perfect for paddlers and swimmers. But it's far more than just somewhere to lay down a towel for the day. A waterfall that runs down onto the beach through an exposed belt of Kimmeridge clay has created a moonscape effect in some sections, and the large boulders and fossils scattered about the sand provide a wonderfully untamed, natural feel. Our suggested walk may be short, but it allows plenty of opportunity to enjoy some spectacular Jurassic Coast views.

BH19 3LL

THE WALK
2.5km / 40mins

BEACH
ACCESS

SY 956,770

THE PITSTOP

A functioning pub since the late 18th century, The Square and Compass in Worth Matravers hasn't changed much in that time. Ales and as many as 13 Wessex ciders may now come from a range of local breweries rather than fermenting barrels in the outhouses, but the way of serving them – through two small hatches – is straight out of the pages of a Thomas Hardy novel. The rambling garden, which looks out over the lush, green hills of the Isle of Purbeck, is dotted with neolithic-like stone tables on which you can rest your pint. While, indoors, the low ceilings, wooden benches and reassuringly tarnished walls have been left exactly as they were in the days when the locals would scan the sea for signs of Napoleonic invasion. The food options are simple: hot pies or pasties. Perfect.

The Square and Compass, Worth Matravers, BH19 3LF. 01929 439229. squareandcompasspub.co.uk

GETTING THERE

- Drive south on the A351 from Corfe Castle and, after a couple of kilometres, turn right onto the B3069 and follow signs to Worth Matravers. Drive through the village, passing the first car park. Follow signs for another car park beyond Weston Farm and leave your car there. Make a donation.

1. Exit the car park through the gate in the wall at the far end.
2. Walk along the path that leads through the field and climb over the stile.
3. Carry on over the brow of the hill and go down the steps directly in front of you. Continue along the steep path and go straight ahead at the crossways, climbing over a stile after around 20 metres. (If the route straight ahead has deteriorated after heavy rain then go left and follow down to beach level that way.)
4. Follow this path as it winds down into a valley and onto the beach.
5. To return, simply retrace your steps.

SUNBATHING 3

SECLUSION 4

SWIMMING 5

SAND 4

ROCKPOOLS & CAVES 3

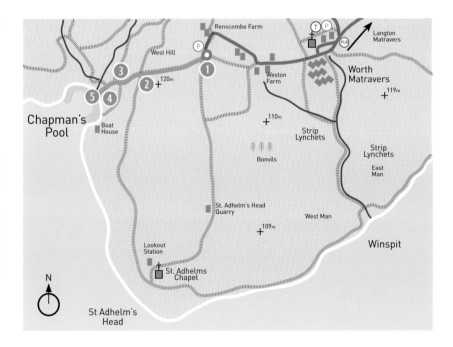

EBB & FLOW

Always accessible, the beach offers large areas of sand at low tide. The curved, well-protected bay is perfect for swimming, as you don't have to worry about currents, undertows or steep shelves.

Somerset

Devon

Dorset

Cornwall

Owned and run by the RSPB, the Arne Nature Reserve is situated on the eastern fringe of the mammoth Poole Harbour and overlooks many of the islands dotted within it. An area of open heath and oak woodland, it is haven for everything from warblers and woodpeckers to owls and ospreys, and deer roam freely among the heather. Our suggested walk to Shipstal Beach, a gorgeous sweep of sand that bleeds into the trees behind, takes you through some classic English woodland, past ponds that teem with frogs and newts, and to a hide from which you can watch the birds that have made their home here.

BH20 5BJ   THE WALK   BEACH   SY 983,882
2.5km / 45mins   ACCESS

EBB & FLOW

Best at high tide, this beach overlooks Long Island and Round Island, to which you can swim when the water's up. As Shipstal Beach is part of a larger estuary, there can be some muddy areas and a fair amount of seaweed at low tide.

THE PITSTOP

Though there's a very good tearoom at Arne Nature Reserve to provide all hot-drink needs – and maybe the occasional KitKat – you should head back to Wareham for greater sustenance. The Old Granary, an imposing former grain house overlooking the River Frome, may have only become a pub in recent years, but its beamed and stone-floored interior provides a reassuringly traditional feel. Hall & Woodhouse Badger is always on tap, along with others from an ever-changing selection of seasonal ales; and the food – as you'd expect from a pub that's part of a small chain – is expertly prepared gastropub fare. Make sure you go for the Stargazy pie, a West Country speciality made from pilchards and pastry, if it's on the menu.

Old Granary, The Quay, Wareham, BH20 4LP. 01929 552010. theoldgranarywareham.co.uk

GETTING THERE

— Drive south out of Wareham on the B3075 and, just as you enter Stoborough, take the left turn onto Nutcrack Lane. Follow this road all the way to the Arne Reserve car park.

1 Walk past the RSPB information hut and turn right just after the picnic area. Follow this path through the woodland.

2 Just after the wooden walkway, turn right and follow the path round until you see Shipstal Beach.

3 Get onto the beach by walking down the access path. Do not climb down any of the sandy slopes. They are very loose and prone to erosion.

4 To continue with our suggested route, carry on along the path, and walk up and over the viewpoint. Turn left onto the track and then right onto the pathway that leads past the ponds. You could opt to take a shortcut back to your car at this point by carrying on along the track rather than turning off.

5 Continue along the path, then take the right-hand fork, which carries on along the pathway through the woods. To visit the hide, turn right over the wooden walkway.

6 Turn right when you meet the track. Follow this all the way to a farm and turn left when you reach the lane. The car park is just a few minutes further along from here.

SUNBATHING

SECLUSION

SWIMMING

SAND

ROCKPOOLS & CAVES

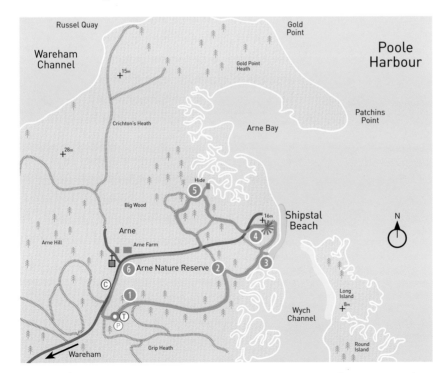

247

INDEX

THE BEACHES

The Arne Nature Reserve, Jurassic Coast	244	Macely Beach, South Devon	198
Avon Estuary, South Devon	190	Marsland Mouth, North Devon	110
Ayrmer Cove, South Devon	186	Meadowsfoot Beach, South Devon	182
		Molunan, South Cornwall	146
Benoath Cove, North Cornwall	94	Moor Sands, South Devon	198
Berry Beach, North Devon	114	Mouthmill Beach, North Devon	118
Booley Beach, South Cornwall	154	Mupe Bay, Jurassic Coast	236
Bosahan Cove, Land's End & the Lizard	14	Nanjizal, Land's End & the Lizard	42
Castle Cove, South Devon	212	Passage Cove, Land's End & the Lizard	14
Cellars Beach, South Devon	178	Pentreath Beach, Land's End & the Lizard	26
Chapman's Pool, Jurassic Coast	240	Polhawn Cove, South Cornwall	170
Cogden Beach, Jurassic Coast	228	Ponsence Cove, Land's End & the Lizard	14
Compass Cove, South Devon	212	Porthallack, Land's End & the Lizard	14
		Porthbeor Beach, South Cornwall	150
Diggory's Island Sand, North Cornwall	74	Porth Chapel, Land's End & the Lizard	38
Doom Bar, North Cornwall	82	Portheras Cove, Land's End & the Lizard	50
Donkey Beach, South Cornwall	166	Porth Joke, North Cornwall	70
Downas Cove, Land's End & the Lizard	22	Porthmeor Cove, Land's End & the Lizard	54
Durgan Beach, Land's End & the Lizard	14	Porth Saxon, Land's End & the Lizard	14
		Prawle Point, South Devon	198
Elender Cove, South Devon	198		
		Ringstead Bay, Jurassic Coast	232
Fishing Cove, North Cornwall	66	Rinsey Beach, Land's End & the Lizard	34
Fox Cove, North Cornwall	78	Rockham Beach, North Devon	122
Frog Prince Cove, South Cornwall	162		
		Shipstal Beach, Jurassic Coast	244
Great Lantic Beach, South Cornwall	158	Soar Mill Cove, South Devon	194
Great Mattiscombe Sand, South Devon	204	Stanbury Mouth, North Cornwall	102
Grebe Beach, Land's End & the Lizard	14	The Strangles, North Cornwall	98
Gwynver, Land's End & the Lizard	46	Swaney Cove, South Devon	178
		Tregardock Beach, North Cornwall	90
Harbour Cove, North Cornwall	82		
Hawker's Cove, North Cornwall	82	Unnamed 1, Land's End & the Lizard	14
Helford Estuary, Land's End & the Lizard	14	Unnamed 2, Land's End & the Lizard	14
Hooken Beach, Jurassic Coast	224		
Housel Cove, Land's End & the Lizard	26	Veor Cove, Land's End & the Lizard	58
Landcombe Cove, South Devon	208	Welcombe Mouth, North Devon	110
Lankidden Cove, Land's End & the Lizard	22	Westcombe Beach, South Devon	186
Lee Bay, North Devon	126	White Nothe Beach, Jurassic Coast	232
Littlecombe Shoot, Jurassic Coast	220	Wild Pear Beach, North Devon	130
Lizard Point, Land's End & the Lizard	26	Woody Bay, North Devon	134
		Wringcliff Bay, North Devon	138

INDEX

THE PITSTOPS

Anchor Inn, Beer, Jurassic Coast — 226
The Apple Tree Community Café & Art Studios,
  Trevescan, Land's End & the Lizard — 44

The Bowgie Inn, West Pentire, North Cornwall — 72
The Bush Inn, Morwenstow, North Cornwall — 104

Cable Station Inn, Porthcurno, Land's End & the Lizard — 40
The Castle Inn, West Lulworth, Jurassic Coast — 238
The Cherub Inn, Dartmouth, South Devon — 214
The Coombe Barton Inn, Crackington Haven,
  North Cornwall — 100
The Cross Keys Inn, Cawsand, South Cornwall — 172

Dartmoor Union, Holbeton, South Devon — 184

The Ferryboat Inn, Helford Passage,
  Land's End & the Lizard — 20
The Foc'c's'le Inn, Combe Martin, North Devon — 132

The Gallery Coffee Shop, Morvah,
  Land's End & the Lizard — 52
The Golden Lion Hotel, Padstow, North Cornwall — 86
The Grampus Inn, Lee, North Devon — 128
The Gurnard's Head, near Zennor,
  Land's End & the Lizard — 56

Hartland Quay Hotel, Hartland, North Devon — 116
Heather's Coffee Shop, Pendeen,
  Land's End & the Lizard — 60
Hive Beach Café, Burton Bradstock, Jurassic Coast — 230
Housel Bay Hotel, Lizard, Land's End & the Lizard — 33
The Hunter's Inn, Heddon Valley, North Devon — 136

The Journey's End Inn, Ringmore, South Devon — 188

The King's Arms, Strete, South Devon — 210
King Arthur's Arms Inn, Tintagel, North Cornwall — 96

The Lion & Lamb, Ashton, Land's End & the Lizard — 36
The Lugger Inn, Polruan, South Cornwall — 160

The Mason's Arms, Branscombe, Jurassic Coast — 222
The Merrymoor Inn, Mawgan Porth, North Cornwall — 76

Mother Meldrum's Tea Room, Valley of Rocks,
  North Devon — 140

The Old Ferry Inn, Bodinnick-by-Fowey,
  South Cornwall — 164
Old Granary, Wareham, Jurassic Coast — 246
The Old Smithy Inn, Darracott, North Devon — 112
The Old Success Inn, Sennen Cove,
  Land's End & the Lizard — 48

The Paris Hotel, Coverack, Land's End & the Lizard — 24
Pig's Nose Inn, East Prawle, South Devon — 200
The Point, Hartland Point, North Devon — 120
Polpeor Café, Lizard, Land's End & the Lizard — 33

The Rashleigh Inn, Polkerris, South Cornwall — 156
Red River Inn, Gwithian, North Cornwall — 68
Ringstead Bay Kiosk, Ringstead, Jurassic Coast — 234
The Rising Sun, St Mawes, South Cornwall — 152

St Anthony Head Tea Garden, St Anthony Head,
  South Cornwall — 148
The Ship Aground, Mortehoe, North Devon — 124
The Ship Inn, Noss Mayo, South Devon — 180
The Shipwright Arms, Helford,
  Land's End & the Lizard — 20
The Sloop Inn, Bantham, South Devon — 192
Smugglers Rest, Talland Bay, South Cornwall — 168
The Soar Mill Cove Hotel, near Salcombe,
  South Devon — 196
The Square and Compass, Worth Matravers,
  Jurassic Coast — 242
The Strand Café, Trebarwith Strand, North Cornwall — 92

The Top House Inn, Lizard, Land's End & the Lizard — 32
The Tradesman's Arms, Stokenham, South Devon — 206
The Tredea Inn, Porthcothan, North Cornwall — 80

The Victory Inn, St Mawes, South Cornwall — 148

The Witchball, Lizard, Land's End & the Lizard — 32

BEST BEACHES FOR...

...SWIMMING

	page
Portheras Cove	50
Diggory's Island Sand	74
Woody Bay	134
Frog Prince Cove	162
Meadowsfoot Beach	182
Mupe Bay	236

...SUNBATHING

	page
Helford Estuary (north shore)	14
Porth Chapel	38
Porth Joke	70
Diggory's Island Sand	74
Great Lantic Beach	158
Elender Cove (Prawle Point)	198

...SURFING

	page
Pentreath Beach (Lizard Point)	26
The Strangles	98
Welcombe Mouth	110
Porthbeor Beach	150
Ayrmer Cove	186
Ringstead Bay (White Nothe)	232

...SUNSETS

	page
Veor Cove	58
Tregardock Beach	90
Rockham Beach	122
Molunan	146
Ayrmer Cove	186
Chapman's Pool	240

...SECLUSION & NATURISM

	page
Veor Cove	58
Fishing Cove	66
The Strangles	98
Wild Pear Beach	130
Landcombe Cove	208
Hooken Beach	224

...CAVES & ROCKPOOLS

	page
Downas Cove	22
Nanjizal	42
Benoath Cove	94
Mouthmill Beach	118
Molunan	146
Castle Cove	212

BEST BEACHES FOR...

...PUBS

	page
Doom Bar	82
Stanbury Mouth	102
Welcombe Mouth	110
Booley Beach	154
Prawle Point	198
Hooken Beach	224

...WILDLIFE & GEOLOGY

	page
Helford Estuary	14
Tregardock Beach	90
Mouthmill Beach	118
Molunan	146
Great Mattiscombe Sand	204
Arne Nature Reserve	244

...LONG HIKES

	page
Lizard Point	26
Tregardock Beach	90
Welcombe Mouth	110
Polhawn Cove	170
Swaney Cove	178
White Nothe Beach	232

...VIEWPOINTS

	page
Lizard Point	26
Diggory's Island Sand	74
Wringcliff Bay	138
Great Lantic Beach	158
Westcombe Beach	186
Prawle Point	198

...FAMILIES

	page
Helford Estuary	14
Doom Bar	82
Rockham Beach	122
Molunan	146
Meadowsfoot Beach	182
Chapman's Pool	240

...SHORT WALKS

	page
Gwynver	46
Portheras Cove	50
Doom Bar	82
Lee Bay	126
Frog Prince Cove	162
Meadowsfoot Beach	182

ABOUT THE AUTHOR

Rob Smith, founder of the Secret Seeker guidebook series, has always had a love of walking, which stems from long summer holidays spent in southwest England as a child. In his late teens he moved to France to follow his passion for cooking, working his way up from *plongeur* to chef at a variety of restaurants. He travelled leisurely from Provence to Paris before returning to the UK in 1996 to establish *The Shoreditch Map*. This monthly listings magazine, for which he wrote about venues and events across the stylish London neighbourhood, ran for over sixty issues before he passed it on as a successful enterprise.

Now, nine years after researching *Secret Beaches: Southwest England*, Rob has published nine more books – see opposite page. After a stint living in the Balearics, where he published five books and founded a walking association, he now lives in Margate, Kent. Rob is thoroughly enjoying developing the Secret Seeker brand and guidebook series. Watch this space!

ACKNOWLEDGEMENTS

Rob would like to say a huge thank you to Rufus Purdy for his editorial superpowers. As well as being an unflappable editor, he's also a talented and inspiring food and travel writer.

Thanks also go to the following for their support, advice, encouragement, hospitality, laughter and friendship: Catriona, Becky, Katy and Daniel; Bogie and Lydia; Pat and Andy; Amie and Leo; Anne and Nic; Tony and Brad.

Big thanks, too, to all those who gave tips on hidden beaches and everyone who opened up their land for camping during the many research trips. And, last but not least, thanks to those who gave much-appreciated comments on the many emails sent out asking for feedback on design predicaments. You know who you are.